SEASONS OF THE SOUL

SEASONS

Nancy Peerman

of the SOUL

The Adventure of Being Human
. . . and Christian

WORD BOOKS, *Publisher*
Waco, Texas • London, England

To my children

The poems which appear at the beginning of several of the chapters of this book are the work of the author.

CONTENTS

Part
One

THE SEASONS
OF THE SOUL

For everything there is a season,
and a time for every matter under heaven . . . .
He has made everything beautiful in its
time; also he has put eternity into man's mind,
yet so that he cannot find out what God has
done from the beginning to the end.

ECCLESIASTES 3:1, 11

"AND THEY LIVED
HAPPILY EVER AFTER."

I'M A HUMAN BEING. THIS MEANS I HAVE problems. It's exciting to be alive, but it's perplexing, too. I'm also a Christian. This offers me hope. I have God's promise that what I am now is not all that I one day will be. But I'm human enough to want the happy ending now, the neat resolution of the dilemmas and conflicts of living.

Yet, as I look around this world in which I live, I find that the rhythm of change is the heartbeat of life. Unceasingly the seasons turn, spring green yields to summer sun, then fades to autumn gold. Nature insists upon her cycle of destruction and renewal, transformation and evolution. Am I not also a creature of change? I must acknowledge birth and death, joy and pain—my seasons of the soul.

Within the limitations and demands of natural surroundings I work out the details of my everyday existence—touching, tasting, hearing, breathing. But I also live in another realm, the boundaries of which are lost from memory. Here hides the child I once was, the person I am to become, my secret self. My body finds its home in the world of the senses; my soul must live beyond. In this far corner of reality I catch a glimpse of the truth about myself.

In every age human needs and difficulties have continued to be the same, different perhaps in specifics, but alike in kind. Love, fear, violence, forgiveness—the moral problem of self-centeredness has not changed since the first man. But the technological efficiency of the twentieth century has infected many of us with the feeling that human beings ought to be perfected in a very short time. For contemporary Christians the dilemma is acute. We face the problem of continuing sin, of knowing what is right and doing what is wrong.

Somehow, the life of the person related to God ought to be a glorious thing, all climbing mountains and no sloughing around in muddy swamps. The Christian can rejoice that his Lord has set things right for mankind and perhaps can feel that he will no longer be plagued by fear or doubt or anxiety or hate. He is sure that with the power of God at work inside him he will soon be freed from the bad habits and psychological problems of a lifetime. So for the Christian, then, the varied experiences that are his can be especially painful. He cannot corner happiness; he is never exempt from tragedy.

But it would seem that we who are Christians should be able to eliminate conflict, at least among ourselves. In the Gospels Christ again and again points the way to peace and understanding, to God's people living in harmony in a loving world. But who among us can stand up and say he has managed to set right his own relationships? Is there a human being who can lead us into freedom of purpose, to happiness and wholeness of personality? Each of us is as bound by our self-centeredness as Lazarus was by his grave clothes. Who can set us free?

I believe that the One who sets people free has already come into the mainstream of human experience. He touched the dead man Lazarus, and He brought him back to life after friends and family had buried him. And the message of the Gospel asserts that His touch is life-giving, even today. But Lazarus could not loose himself from the winding cloth, so Jesus commanded his friends, "Unbind him, and let him go" (John 11:44). The man who had been brought back to life still was not free.

Here, then, is the paradox of the Christian life. Why do I continue to fall short, to misunderstand, to separate myself from God and man? Knowing from my past experience the goodness of God's grace, why do I struggle on by myself, sometimes to sure defeat? What is it in me that wars against what I know to be in my own best interest? Why is the Christian life begun and not ended at the climax of conversion? I want the happy ending now! Oh, God, why must I be so everlastingly human!

DICHOTOMY

Mirror of my being,
Ancient antagonist from womb to grave,
And on beyond?

Conflict bloodless,
With small passion, unresolved;
Each seeks the final blessing.

I do not understand my own actions. For I do not what I want, but I do the very thing I hate.

ROMANS 7:15

"WELL, YOU'VE DONE IT AGAIN!" THE ACCUS-
ing voice was all the more scornful because
it was my own, inside. At this point I wished with all my
heart that I could turn the clock back a few moments, but
from the tightened lines in my son's face I knew that what
was done was done. In anger I had struck out to hurt someone I loved. Now he and I had to pay the price of my
quick temper.

I begged his pardon. Already I knew how wrong I had
been. And after a few tears and some calmer talk, we settled back into the warmth of our accustomed relationship.
But the little voice continued to whisper to me, "You really
are a stinker, aren't you! Why did you blow up? You
aren't a Christian. Christians don't do that!" The truth

stung me and I thought, "That's right. I'll never make it as a Christian. I might just as well give up now, because I'll never be able to control what I do, much less what I think."

It seemed that I was back where I started, haunted by an impossible ideal of personal perfection. I had grown up with some unrealistic ideas about my own nature. Religion was ritual; God was remote, the object of mystic adoration. The poetry and novels that I read tended to be romantic, mainly in the vein of the nobility of man. I adopted the philosophy of my father, a politically hopeful man. In spite of two world wars in his lifetime he felt that there were still solutions to man's age-old problem of violence. Society, given enough time, could produce the ideal man.

The result of these influences was that I expected far too much of myself and those around me. I very early denied myself (and others) the right to be human. As I grew older disillusionment set in and I could not avoid the knowledge that there was something wrong with the world. At the age of twenty-nine I was crushed by the realization that no matter how hard I tried I could not live a good life. My helplessness brought me to the absolute necessity of surrender to God. Finally I accepted His offer of a new kind of life. I turned around, and, acknowledging Christ as Savior, I set out in a new direction.

This beginning again was a wonderful experience for me. As time passed, I could see in my life the results of God's Holy Spirit at work in me to change the kind of person I was. But I had to admit that I wasn't a perfect

18

Christian. I still felt anger, hostility, hate. I continued to do destructive things to those I loved.

Temptation comes in subtle ways. The fourth chapter of Matthew describes the period Jesus spent in the desert, fasting and praying, in preparation for His active ministry. The devil appeared to Him there and offered his services, as a shortcut to power and glory. Satan said, in effect, "Look, You don't have to go through all this—the pain of rejection, the humiliation of crucifixion. I'll give you dominion over all the world. All you have to do is bow down and worship me!"

"Begone, Satan!" Jesus replied, "for it is written, 'You shall worship the Lord your God and him only shall you serve!' "

In essence, my temptation was the same. A soft voice said to me, "You want to be perfect *right now!* You don't want to have to go through sadness and boredom and pain, learning to do things God's way. Surrender. Give up your faith in Christ. See, He hasn't made a difference in you. You're the same old Nancy!" It didn't sound like the power of evil, but if I could have been persuaded that I could not be a Christian, then Satan would have won the day. Perhaps it seems naïve to claim reality for Satan, but I do acknowledge the existence of a dark spirit at work in the world, by whatever name he is called. And I must reckon that I am prey to the power and suggestion of evil. I had been tempted to deny what Christ could do for me, and I might have given up then, except that my relationship to Him did not depend on me alone. His love held me though I wanted to run away.

19

This was a rough time for me, spiritually. I could not shake my guilt over the fact that I was letting God down. But not long after, my husband and I attended a weekend conference where we studied the first eight chapters of the Book of Romans. These deal with the Apostle Paul's exposition of sin and man's nature, and God's provision for ultimate victory over evil. I could have shouted for joy as I read the last sentences of chapter seven: "Wretched man that I am! Who will deliver me from this body of death? Thanks be to God through Jesus Christ our Lord! So then, I of myself serve the law of God with my mind, but with my flesh I serve the law of sin." Paul continues wonderfully, opening the eighth chapter with what is surely one of the most positive statements of the Bible— "There is therefore now no condemnation for those who are in Christ Jesus."

He didn't say sin; he said condemnation. And I saw that the reason there was no condemnation was the *position* I had with God because of the Lord Jesus Christ and His sacrifice on the Cross. At the moment I accepted Him, acknowledging that of myself I could not be right with God, I was given the righteousness of the Son of God. I could no more continue the Christian life without Him than I could have begun it on my own.

I could now understand that my attempt to live the Christian life in perfection by trying to adhere to a system of do's and do not's was the expression of an enormous amount of pride, for what I was really saying was, "Thank you, Lord Jesus, for saving me. Now I believe I can finish up on my own!" It was the problem of self again.

Just as I began by trusting in the power of Christ, so must I continue, relying on His goodness in me, in order that I might change into the kind of person He would have me be.

Now there is not a doubt in my mind that in eternity I will be a perfected creature. Jesus said, "You, therefore, must be perfect, as your heavenly Father is perfect" (Matthew 5:48). This means to me, in loose paraphrase, "You ought to be perfect, for that is the way God is and the only way to be." Only the spirit of Christ within me can aspire to such a goal. It humbles me to admit I need His help; but as I realize my own dependence, I can understand that others share my weakness—the problem of being human.

Very early in the development of the Christian Church, theologians sought to deal with the question of spiritual man and natural man. Can they coexist, or must one be negated? To some it seemed an either/or proposition. One sect, the Gnostics, concluded that all matter was evil and must be denied. Carried to its extreme conclusion, this theory became heresy, for the humanity of Christ had to be eliminated from their system of theology. Men and women under the influence of this concept of the evils of the flesh went off by themselves in caves, dressing in rags and eating only enough to keep skin and bones together.

Asceticism had its day in the Church, for those rare souls who could pay the price. But I think that today we see the absurdity of trying to live as though we are not human at all, as though man is some sort of spirit chained to the confines of an evil body. It is a mockery of God's

21

Creation to claim that everything material is bad and everything spiritual is good. In the Gospel of Matthew, Christ himself deals with the issue in speaking to the Pharisees about their elaborate rituals concerning eating. As He points out, it is not what goes into the body but what comes out of the heart that makes man sinful (Matthew 15:17–20).

But the controversy has raged through the centuries and the standards of the Christian world have fluctuated with the ascendancy of one point of view or the other. Today it seems that the emphasis has shifted to positive Christian involvement in the world as opposed to the idea of avoiding contamination by it. Unhappily, though, we of the Church are not as free from the asceticism of the Puritan standard as we perhaps would like to think.

One of the most terrible things that Christians do to each other is to render judgment about another's behavior. A person who calls himself "Christian" finds himself open to all sorts of comments. "Well, I know some people who work for him and they don't think he's all that great!" Or, "If she's really a Christian, why don't I see her down at the church more often?" These whispers are the echoes of the voices with which we condemn ourselves. Some of us blind ourselves to our own shortcomings by focusing on the obvious sins of our brothers in Christ. Not one of us, though, can stand measurement against the yardstick of perfection.

Even Christian heroes, like other idols, prove to be entirely human. It liberates me to realize that we are all made of the same stuff; wholeness is a matter of degree.

22

I feel certain that the impact of Christians in the everyday world would be far greater if we beat our critics to the punch and openly confessed that we are not perfect. They certainly find it out about us, anyway. And after all, our real witness is to God's goodness, not our own.

"What shall we say then? Are we to continue in sin that grace may abound? By no means!" (Romans 6:1,2). There is much that I need to understand about the dual nature I possess, although I am sure that the issue will not be perfectly resolved in this lifetime of mine. I certainly cannot relax comfortably with my allotted sins and figure all will be well in the long run. I am not excused from sin, far from it. As I understand the paradox of sin and grace, it seems that my part in my re-creation is not to make myself over, but to give God permission to do so. I own my own house, so to speak, and God will not infringe on my rightful ownership. But He wants to remodel the structure, patch the leaky roof, improve on the design. I must trust that He has my very best interest at heart in whatever work and bother and discomfort is involved for me. How hard it is for me to believe that He really loves me!

I have all sorts of excuses about why He can't do much with me. After all, consider my circumstances. If I didn't have so much housework to do, I'd have time to be a better neighbor. If I didn't have allergies, I wouldn't be so cross. If I had as much money as "they" do, I'd tithe, too. Each of us has his given set of circumstances, and I am sure most of us like some of them and want to change others. I envy others a few of their special gifts, but I wonder if

23

I'd like their total packages any better than my own. It would be very nice to possess the beauty of a certain film star, but I know I wouldn't like to take on her three divorces and several assorted sets of children.

Do circumstances have the final say as to what we are to become? A friend of mine, a surgeon, has a favorite saying—"The facts don't count." I asked him what he meant, and in reply, he told me a story.

As a new Christian, he felt that he wanted to bring Christ into his medical practice. A short time before, he had found help for his own problems in the context of turning to God. Now he wanted to share with others the reality he had found. In spite of the obvious amusement of some of his colleagues, he found the courage to pray before operations, and he began to commit his skill and the outcome of his surgery to the will of God.

One such operation was an attempt to repair the circulatory system in a man's leg. From the beginning it went badly, with all sorts of complications. Finally, though, the surgeon completed the intricate reconstruction with reasonable success. During the patient's lengthy convalescence he and the doctor began to talk about life, about what gave meaning to it all. My friend shared with his patient something of his own experience with Christ, and one of the nurses on the case brought the man a Bible and read to him. Then, suddenly, infection flared in the leg. The only thing the doctor could do was to amputate it. He was heartsick. He had put his trust in God—and now he wasn't at all sure that God hadn't let him down.

Several weeks later his patient came to his office for a

final checkup. As he was leaving in his wheelchair, he paused a moment, and then he said, "Listen, doc, I know you feel bad about my leg. I do, too. But I want to tell you something. I'm stronger now in lots of ways, than I was before." He added, "You know, now that Christ is in my life, there's a reason to live." For this man, the facts really didn't count.

Many gallant people do live beyond the limitations of a situation. Sometimes, though, we don't want to. Why does a child with an IQ of 140 fail in school? Perhaps it is because he needs the attention he can get in no other way. His need insures his failure. A talented man bounces from job to job, always finding fault with the current position, always seeking another. Are the jobs really the problem? And surely Alcoholics Anonymous has demonstrated that until a person faces his compulsion and wants to change the pattern, he will continue to drink, even if (or perhaps because) his drinking will ruin his life in the long run.

I think this is in part what Paul meant about doing what you would not. Psychologically speaking, there are forces at work in each of us about which we know very little, but which nevertheless dictate many of our responses. A number of years ago I spent some time in psychotherapy, and one of the most valuable insights that I got about myself was an understanding of the principle of self-defeating behavior. I learned that I loved failure.

Early in our marriage, for instance, my husband and I fell into a pattern that we followed whenever we disagreed about something. My first reaction was to try to hide the fact that our opinions were different. I pretended to go along with Bob because I wanted his approval. Then I slowly boiled inside, and when sufficient pressure had built up, I erupted. He would of course be surprised; he had thought the matter was settled. His response to my anger was to defend himself. I took his defense as a personal attack and the battle was on. It always ended with my being in tears, apologizing and insisting that he was right. I *never* won an argument—not because he wouldn't let me, but because I had decided before the argument even began that I would go down in defeat. I wanted to lose, for then I could justify feeling sorry for myself. For some reason I had the need to experience emotional pain. It took a lot of talking out and thinking over this pattern to realize that many of my actions were programed to offer me the opportunity to feel hurt.

As I began to see some of my problems, I tried to excuse myself by saying that these were patterns established very early in my life. After all, it couldn't be my fault; I had always been that way. My psychiatrist annoyed me by continually bringing me back to the present. He'd say, "I know that you have always had a problem expressing strong feelings. But what are you going to do about it now, today, tomorrow?" Every time I tried to duck the responsibility for changing, he gently brought me back to the possibility that I could learn to react differently, that I could decline to enter into self-defeating behavior, that the same situation could produce a new response from me. It was harder to do it his way, but I began to learn freedom as I gained the courage to experiment a little with my own behavior. I found that the world didn't end if I disagreed with Bob and that real love is not as fragile as I had supposed.

It is sometimes the path of least resistance to remain immature emotionally. It is easier to live a narrow, accustomed way, more comfortable to set up standards of behavior which are predictable and which offer a measure of success. (I haven't ever killed anyone; I haven't committed adultery; I wouldn't take anything that doesn't belong to me.) If I understand the Sermon on the Mount at all, I must realize that the standards posed in it deal with what is inside my heart as well as with what I do in the world. This is the point at which understanding of my own psychology comes to the fore as an important part of the way I mature as a Christian, for to become an adult in Christ, to grow up in Him in the sense of making a mature, loving response to the situations of life requires examination and consideration of the motives and feelings below the surface of my actions.

Emotional maturity is not a static state. This is often brought home to me as I try to understand my own children. At dinner one evening our five-year-old daughter finished quickly, was excused, and skipped outside to play on the trampoline before it got dark. After she had gone, her brother, who was eleven, exclaimed. "That Jennifer! Boy, is she ever spoiled! She won't ever take turns right on the trampoline." His older brother chimed in, "Yeah, why does she always have to have her own way?" As Bob and I talked with them we all agreed that Jennifer's behavior was often self-centered. Then my husband asked the boys if they could remember how they had felt about sharing when they had been only five. They could not, but I certainly did. I had to laugh as I recalled all the refereeing I had done in the cause of justice. But I could also see that they had matured to the point that they didn't like the fussing and snatching so natural to younger children. And at that particular moment I was encouraged as a parent!

I reflected later, though, that some people just don't mature beyond a certain point. I thought about an older woman I know who cannot bear to relinquish the center of the conversation; about a man who pouts for days if his wife crosses him; about a teacher who shrieks at the children in her class in the name of discipline. It requires great courage to continue to grow emotionally, because we have to recognize unpleasant things about ourselves sometimes. We often decline to pay the price. It may be that we need help to struggle through the jungle of tangled feelings, twisted motives, and stifled guilts that bar our path. But Christ talked about walking in the light and even the dimmest light is better than the dark.

A QUESTION
OF IDENTITY

"By 'identification' we mean the act or process of becoming like something or someone in one or several aspects of thought or behavior."

CHARLES BRENNER, M.D.

Beloved, we are God's children now; it does not yet appear what we shall be, but we know that when he appears we shall be like him, for we shall see him as he is.

I John 3:2

THE QUESTION OF IDENTITY BEGINS IN THE
crib. The human infant first understands reality in relation to his own body. The sensation of being
involves two distinct aspects—feeling and being felt. A
baby's own hand is more wonderful to him than any other
hand in the world; he can feel other objects with it, and
he can experience the feeling of the hand itself.

Of course more complex explorations of identity occur
as a child becomes conscious of not only his own body and
its sensations but the physical and emotional response of
those around him. Other people tell him about himself.
His mother, if she gratifies his needs, assures him thereby
of his value. The process of identification, which psychology defines as the act of becoming like something or someone, has begun, with tremendous implications in terms of

the emotional development of that child. But beyond identification with other human beings, what is it that defines individual uniqueness? What differentiates one life from all those other billions of lives which share this planet Earth?

In the normal everyday course of life our close and accustomed relationships give shape to our idea of who we are. Members of our family, our friends, the people with whom we work—all of these are important in establishing the boundaries of personality. In the event of an abrupt interruption of the usual pattern of our lives we suffer a sense of disorientation. The death of someone close to us changes, inevitably, an area of reality for us. The daughter-father relationship ceased to be part of reality for me when my father died, and I had to reevaluate who I was in the light of what I had lost.

Even a change of scene can cause me to feel unsure of my identity. In the speed of the jet age I can find myself far from my usual surroundings in a few hours. On my first visit to New York City several years ago, I felt acutely anxious shortly after my arrival. I wasn't sure why. As I thought about my anxiety, I realized that I had been plucked from my familiar routine and had been set down in a whirling world of new sounds, unfamiliar faces, uncommon sights. On the streets of New York I passed hundreds of people without the slightest flicker of recognition from any of them. No one knew that I was Nancy Peerman. I wondered, "Who am I really, apart from my home, my children, my neighbors? I could be anybody, as far as these people around me are concerned!"

But as I struggled with my feelings, I was aware that I did have an identity which did not change with my surroundings. I sensed that deep inside was the real me, part of the creative life force which we call God. My identity rested with Him, for He had created me. As the compass needle points to magnetic north, so did my security depend on acknowledgment of the basis of my being. And, suddenly, I was at home in the strangeness of New York City.

Perhaps by nature I am more given to introspection than many people, but I suspect that at times all of us have wondered about ourselves, about who we really are. Psychology, a fairly recent addition to the sciences, was developed as a result of intense curiosity about the behavior of man, about what really goes on in the mind of the human being. Because of the problem of measuring and cataloguing human emotional response it has been difficult to gather knowledge in this field, but much important work was done in the early years of this century by Sigmund Freud. It is true that he outraged people with his radical ideas about the sexual nature of man. (Even today his name is a dirty word to some—I have a friend who pronounces his last name "Fraud," and she means it!) Although there are many areas of disagreement about his conclusions, even among professionals in the field of psychology, Freud did provide a body of knowledge which has proved to be sound through several generations of experimentation. Some of us would like that knowledge to vanish. It is an uncomfortable thought, for example, that we are not in complete control of our emotions and actions.

33

Freud described the human mind as being divided into three functioning parts—the id, the ego, and the superego.

". . . the *id* comprises the psychic representatives of the drives, the *ego* consists of those functions which have to do with the individual's relation to his environment, and the *superego* comprises the moral precepts of our minds as well as our ideal aspirations."[1]

The id is present at birth, a collection of drives, urges, and psychic tensions. This is the raw material of personality. From the id develops the ego, during the first six or eight months of life. The self-absorbed infant becomes a social being. The superego does not arise until the child is six or seven years old. Almost any parent can verify that the small child doesn't have a strong sense of right and wrong until about that age. For centuries children were regarded as miniature adults, expected to fit adult standards of behavior. Now, to say that the raw material of personality is present at birth is not to imply that what we are to become is fixed. Psychologists can demonstrate the effects of environment on development.

I envision my own trio of id, ego, and superego as a sort of three-dimensional chess set—I make moves on all three levels at the same time. Id says, "Do it now! Never mind the consequences, I *want* to!" Superego replies, "Oh, you mustn't! I won't allow it!" In the meantime poor ego is squashed between the two opposing forces, crying, "Help! Can't we work this out?" But in spite of the ob-

1. Charles Brenner, *An Elementary Textbook of Psychoanalysis* (New York: International Universities Press, 1955; reprint ed., Doubleday, 1957), p. 38.

vious conflicts which go on inside most of the time, we do work things out. Emotional disturbance ensues when the balance of power is upset. A strangling superego can leave a person incapable of action, afraid of making a mistake. A raging id can be like the devils of hell set loose, to the ultimate destruction of self.

To complicate matters further, the triune personality functions at several different levels of awareness. It stores experiences, information, and memories in one of three different places. First, there is the conscious, what is being thought about right now. Next is the preconscious, that material which is readily available to be brought forward to the conscious. Finally there is the unconscious, the burying ground for what is barred from conscious thought, that which is "forgotten." It is not necessary to understand the whys of the three levels of consciousness. It is enough to know that at a given moment there is more going on in the mind than we are aware of. Why some incidents in the past remain vivid while others pass from recollection is not the real question, unless we suffer emotional disability and need professional help. It is in order to enjoy a measure of understanding of ourselves that we need to be aware of the way we really operate. We must understand that we are not in full control of the forces within us.

As one who has done only limited reading in the area of psychology, I can comprehend these theories in merely a general way. I have my own system of describing the aspects of my identity—and this is strictly a personal view, intuitive rather than scientific. As I think about myself, I realize that there is a Nancy who is seen casually by other people—the one who goes to the grocery store, picks up carpool, attends meetings. A more intimate glimpse of me is the one that my friends and family have, for I share with them, willingly or unwillingly, more of who I really am. Just ask my children what I'm really like! Beyond this layer is another, a place I reserve for myself alone. Here I think my secret thoughts and add to my storehouse of dreams and desires. This is a world of fantasy. Some parts of it I eventually act out, but much of it remains hidden. This is the heart, into which Christ sees so clearly.

But, I think there is a deeper level yet. Beneath the layer of my private world is the most secret dwelling place of my soul, where the Holy Spirit works, as God's agent, in the shaping of the eternal me, the new creation of which Paul speaks in II Corinthians. God means me to live with Him someday, and I must be made fit for such a life. "Likewise the Spirit helps us in our weakness; for we do not know how to pray as we ought, but the Spirit himself intercedes for us with sighs too deep for words" (Romans 8:26).

Why, then, this analyzing of the human soul? What is the profit in self-knowledge, even if you have it? I think it lies in the fact that as we understand something of our own nature, we are willing to let God change us. I cannot believe there is a person on earth, at least among those who claim sanity, who would say that he was already a perfected creature. We are all of us, Christian or not, subject to the divine order of human nature, which means that each of us harbors the *potential* for any sin and every virtue. There are no new sins, only variations of the same ones experienced by earliest man. Nor is there a sin each of us is not capable of committing, given conditions that push us to the moral limits of our being. What would my actions be, if my family were thrust into the nightmare of a concentration camp? To what limits would I go to see that my children had enough to eat? Or were protected from abuses? As just a human being, I know what I would probably do; God Himself knows the strength that He alone could impart to me under such circumstances. In other words, we who congratulate ourselves on the fine quality of our lives need only reflect a little on our good fortune and on Jesus' words—"Those who are well have no need of a physician, but those who are sick; I came not to call the righteous, but sinners" (Mark 2:17).

Most of us are misfits by somebody's standards—I look askance at hippies and they despise me for being "establishment." We seek out for company those who are like us—politically, socially, and economically. We are a little bit afraid of those who differ from us, but the range of what we can call normal behavior is rather wide. One of the interesting statements that I found in Dr. Brenner's text dealt with the line which separates normal and abnormal behavior. He holds the opinion that "there is not a wide gulf between the normal and the psychoneurotic, but that, on the contrary, the psychological differences between them are ones of degree rather than kind."[2]

We share the burden of our humanity. We need to learn that it is no good telling an emotion-ridden human

2. *Ibid.*, p. 200.

being to "shape up." We need to understand that he is riding one wild horse after another, perhaps to his destruction, and to try to find the means to help him. As Christians, the hope that we share with the world of disturbed and broken people is God's promise in Christ that what we are now is not all that we shall be, one day. But part of the cost is that we must see ourselves as we are in order that we may become something more. Self-knowledge can be a painful proposition; Jesus warned us to count the cost of becoming an authentic person—a complete individual, whole in the sense of being one with God.

People have always longed for authenticity in life. They search today for meaning in a world which suddenly seems a bit too much to cope with. Not many of us who live in this complex age are really as interested in eventual salvation from a traditional hell as we are in getting through the problems of today and next week. For we are children of our time, and there is a quality of immediacy about this era of ours. It is the now, and not the hereafter, which tantalizes us with the question of existence. •

And man is afraid of himself; he has power to work miracles, but he lacks responsible knowledge of how to use those miracles. He cannot bear to be left to his own devices, and his alienation from self and others prompts escape into alcohol, drugs, sexual license, violence. He substitutes these to avoid coming to terms with the problem of existence. In the United States today we are plagued with conditions that seem beyond our control; we feel that we have lost our heritage. In spite of our best efforts things seem to be going downhill; some of us try to build our own small world and keep it safe for the future, praying that it will not be swept away by a catastrophe beyond our control.

But the search for authentic life does not stop because we are afraid of the future. While we recognize the presence of the quality of authenticity in some of the lives of the people we admire—the special ones we call "geniuses" or "stars" or "heroes"—we fail to see how it was achieved or what inspiration it can afford us. We are awed by the talent of a Rubinstein or the incredible achievements of an Einstein or the athletic records of a Babe Ruth. These people seem larger than life—exceptional—and perhaps they are. But they also are those who have accepted their own potential as the guideline for their development and have worked to reach their own outer limits of ability. They have chosen the principle of disciplined effort as their commitment—to do whatever they want to do most the best that they can, whatever the cost. There are far more "geniuses" around than we recognize; indeed, most of us fail to see our own capacity for the authenticity of genius.

Every great work of art has about it a sense of completeness. It is a whole; it hangs together in terms of color, balance, harmony, interest. Just as the patterns of a Bach fugue are resolved in unity, so do the elements of an authentic life have structure. The authentic woman will always be more than the sum of the roles she assumes—wife, mother, executive, poet, dishwasher. She may be brain or beauty, or just plain ordinary, but underneath it all she is a *woman*. And she must recognize that it is this fact that

39

lends unity and authenticity to her life, however she lives it. The authentic Christian is stamped with the quality of life lived by Christ, superimposed on the human personality.

To be effective in today's world the Christian Church must recognize man's need for wholeness and must offer the unique answer of the Christian faith to the fragmentation and confusion of modern life. The good news of Christianity is that it offers not just doctrine, but a chance for authentic life in relationship with that most perfect personality of all time, Jesus of Nazareth. He knew who He was. He was the Son of God, and it was this understanding of the basis of His existence here on earth that gave validity to every action of His life. He was not the patchwork of good and bad that the rest of us are, but a whole person. It is to the end of wholeness and fulfillment for every human being that He offered up His life, for He knew that apart from God man is always incomplete.

It pushes the limits of my present understanding to try to grasp the full meaning of what Christ has done for me on the Cross. Sometimes I want to just settle for the comfortable knowledge I already possess. As a Christian, continuing along the road, I am sometimes frightened to leave behind the familiar, to stretch beyond my present maturity. In trying to fathom my own being, am I moving further away or closer to God? Or am I moving at all? I write about being an authentic person, but who am I, really?

For many years of my life I sought to find a wise man who could tell me what I wanted to know about myself.

40

Several times I thought I had found him, but I have come to the conclusion that the most that human beings can do for each other is to trade misinformation and to share an occasional glimpse of what is true and eternal. I know now that for me there can be no wise man, but only God, He who knows. Man's strong sense of fatalism about life can only be resolved in God. Why life, and in the midst of life, death? The question must be asked, but is there an answer? I surrendered my future to God when I could no longer bear to live without an affirmation to the question of existence.

We are not living simply to get through our allotted years—something happens to us in the living, for better or for worse. We either become more complete or more fragmented. When we are young the alternatives seem endless, but in making each successive choice—occupation, marriage, parenthood—we narrow the real possibilities. The fact that I am married to a husband who lives in Texas precludes my taking a job in San Francisco. Each of us is limited by his own set of circumstances, of course, but sometimes these very same restrictions of life produce the pressure necessary for creative living. Recently I was talking with a young artist, a fine watercolorist who is rapidly making a name for himself. I asked him if he were looking forward to the day when he could afford to give up his job as a newspaper cartoonist and paint full-time. He laughed a little and said, "You know, I had three weeks' vacation last summer and I thought I'd paint all the time. I did, too, for the first week. Then I began sleeping late, and since I didn't have to go to the newspaper, I didn't even shave. By the end of the third week I was an unproductive slob!"

Because I want very much to write, and write well, my domestic responsibilities weigh heavily on me at times. I think, "Oh, to have a little shack somewhere, with the children running around barefooted, and no homework to help with and everyone eating sandwiches off paper plates. Then maybe I'd have time to write!" But I laugh as I remind myself that I typed the manuscript of my first book to the strains of the Tijuana Brass, with my three-year-old daughter hanging over the back of my chair! How many times we are tempted to put off doing things until there is more time, less confusion, greater income. Before we know it we have settled for a style of living that is less than our potential. A person who says in all humility, "Oh, I could never do that!" may be correctly assessing his limitations, but he also may be denying the creativity of God. The real waste in human terms is often potential that is never realized.

Few people dare to be original. It is too risky; in man the herd instinct is strong. It is safe in the middle of the crowd, but, standing apart, a person is vulnerable and perhaps a little lonely. Jesus certainly knew the price of being different; He felt the sting of rejection. But if the creative effort of God, which produces a unique human being each and every time, is to be fulfilled, then His children must have the courage to find the shape of their particular contribution to God's world.

I hesitated a long time before I decided to try to write a book. There have been so many fine books on the Chris-

42

tian life—and besides, who could improve on Paul! But during an art lecture I heard the instructor say, "By this time, in the history of painting, there are no new subjects to paint. Everything's been done." He paused and added, "There are only new painters." The thought flashed through my mind, "No one has told the story of the reality of Christ in an ordinary life from quite my point of view. And it's my own experience—it's original, at least." So I began the very difficult business of learning to communicate, and in that process a new dimension was added to my experience. Perhaps to be an authentic person is as simple as to be oneself—and to be glad of it—for there is a calm that comes in assenting to the kind of person that God means you to be. It is the peace that passes understanding.

THE IMAGE
OF THE UNSEEN

"No one has ever seen psychic energy and no one ever will, any more than any one has ever seen any of the forms of physical energy."

CHARLES BRENNER, M.D.

In the beginning was the Word, and the Word was with God, and the Word was God. He was in the beginning with God; all things were made through him, and without him was not anything made that was made.

JOHN 1:1–3

IN SIMPLE BUT POWERFUL LANGUAGE JOHN
begins his great Gospel account by defining
his concept of the essence of Jesus Christ. He chooses a
particular phrase, "the Word," as the image of God. John
says, in effect, that in the beginning was the essence of
God, Christ, and that He always was, and ever will be
"Very God of very God." [1]

"And the Word became flesh and dwelt among us, full
of grace and truth; we have beheld his glory, glory as of
the only Son from the Father" (John 1:14). In this passage John goes on to testify to the image of God that he

1. The Nicene Creed, *The Book of Common Prayer*, according to the use
of the Protestant Episcopal Church in the United States of America, p. 16.

himself has seen, someone whom John has known as a friend. A characteristic of human thought is that the mind must deal with both the essence and the image, two quite different aspects of an object or person. So John goes further and identifies the two aspects of Christ as one, essence and image in the same person. "No one has ever seen God; the only Son, who is in the bosom of the Father, he has made him known" (John 1:18).

In the duality of man's life, material and spiritual, there are essences and images, neither of which is complete without the other. The essence of love is expressed in the image of love. I show my feeling of love for my little daughter (the essence of affection) by holding her close and whispering, "Jennifer, I love you" (affection made concrete). My love may exist whether I express it or not, but Jennifer understands my feelings for her when I express it visibly. In the same way, God's love for man was made known in the life and death and resurrection of Jesus Christ, the Son who reveals the Father.

Communication between human beings is an example of the difference between essence and image. I can't eat the word "apple" but my mouth waters when I hear someone say the word. My taste buds respond to the image of what I know to be something very good to eat. Our senses react to many images; responses may vary from situation to situation and from individual to individual. One of the problems of communication is that not all of us share the same image for an essence. After all, it is not that the apple changes, but that apples taste different to some people than to others.

The question of images is a very personal one, for I know from experience how images can control my life. I became aware of my personal collection of images as a result of a talk my husband gave at a Campus Crusade meeting several years ago. He analyzed for these college students the number of roles he had assumed in order to impress other people. His manly image required that he go on hunting trips that he didn't enjoy. The authority role of father kept him from admitting to his children that he was ever wrong. The businessman syndrome pushed him to prove himself sharper than his competitors. He went on to say that through his new understanding of himself as a Christian he could see how limiting these roles were, because he spent so much time and energy protecting them.

As I thought of my own roles—efficient homemaker, faithful community worker, charming wife, wise mother— I began to sense that the freedom Christ talked about might be the freedom to be myself, to be able to set aside false ideals in the interest of enjoying the style of life that fits the real me. I began experimenting a little with the way I spent my time and found it surprisingly hard to do, for I think most of us have reasonably iron-clad schedules which seem to be dictated by our circumstances. I discovered that I had to work hard to be flexible, and more amazingly, that the things I did for "fun" I sometimes didn't really want to do. Because I have a golf course at my back door, I assumed I ought to play golf; but consistently taking a sixteen on the same hole convinced me that I was not physically equipped to be a golfer and that my heart wasn't really in it. It finally dawned on me that

I could enjoy *looking* at the beauty of that enormous expanse of green grass without chasing a silly little ball around!

In modern America it seems that the prizes and the accolades go to the producers; and this makes it particularly difficult for the full-time homemaker to enjoy a feeling of satisfaction about the small, repetitious chores that she must do every day. Often the result is that she feels she must have some kind of worthwhile public image in order to be a "success"; hence she throws herself and her time and energy into doing things she really doesn't enjoy. And really, many men suffer from the same compulsion, or worse; they get caught up in what is sometimes referred to as the Protestant work ethic—the spirit of all work and no frivolity. There was a period of almost a year in my husband's life before he became a Christian when he worked seven days a week. Fortunately, he has learned that there is sound logic in the idea of the Sabbath day of rest.

One of the more fascinating aspects of this problem of images is that often one is truly unaware of the way he operates. It is only in the past year that I have begun to see the tremendous competitive streak that I have, and always have had. I took up the game of tennis and found that losing a game was very difficult for me to accept; I wanted to win all my matches. This is not necessarily bad. But very early in my life I began downgrading my efforts in competing with others, using self-effacement as a cover for my competitiveness. I wanted very much to be first in anything that I did, but if I made good grades on my report card, I didn't want anyone to see it. The crippling thing about my desire to excel was that I would not attempt anything that I did not feel sure I could do well. As God has worked in my life, I have begun to recognize this trait; He is freeing me to accept my own potential as a reasonable standard of success. I'll never be asked to play tennis on the pro circuit, but I'm going to learn to play good tennis if it takes ten years. Although the spirit of competition is still very much with me—and I think that's a good thing because it spurs me on—I realize that if I'm to find the limits of my talents, I have to be willing to fail.

The ferment in the Christian Church today—the New Theology, the Lay Renewal, Vatican II, Social Involvement—is perhaps evidence that the Church is more willing to experiment, freer to acknowledge its mistakes. From age to age the images of God have changed as men have sought to pinpoint infinite God. Primitive man believed the essence of God could be contained in a stone idol. Sophisticated man believes that perhaps there is no essence, that God has withdrawn from the world of men or that He never existed in the first place.

Looking back at the development of the Judeo-Christian tradition, it is easy to see how people in each age have interpreted the essence of God in images that were familiar to them. Early believers dealt with the mystery of God in terms of their everyday experience. The Jews, in an unstable political situation, longed for a strong king to offer them protection and stability. The image of God as King has long been part of their religious understanding of Him. The early Christians used the same symbol for the Son of

51

God, as they made Christ the King known to an unbelieving world. "A mighty fortress is our God" had special meaning to people who lived in fear, as wars swept back and forth across Europe.

One of the problems that Christianity faces in this present day is that the Church's images of God seem archaic. The essence of the Trinity—God the Father, God the Son, God the Holy Spirit—has not changed since the foundation of the world, but it may be that our images no longer have meaning for a world that is changing so drastically from one generation to the next.

The twentieth century has been shaped by many things—outstanding among them, science and compounding technology. Ever since Freud rocked the world with his theories about what the human mind is really like we have been heirs of the Age of Psychology. Our understanding of ourselves and other people (and sometimes our lack of understanding) has shaped our laws, our behavior, and even our comprehension of Biblical truth. I do not qualify as even an amateur psychologist, but, like many other people today, I have bathed in watered-down psychology for a long time. I suppose by osmosis I have acquired a certain understanding of human behavior. One of the most exciting discoveries that I made as I began to take the Bible seriously is the psychological soundness of what it says. I had never much liked the part about the sins of the fathers being visited on their children (Exodus 20:5). At first glance the passage would seem to indicate that God is a spiteful God, wreaking revenge forever. Then it dawned on me that the passage was saying exactly the same thing Dr.

Spock says—that as a parent, what I do for and to and with my children has tremendous implications in terms of their well-being.

It seems to me that thoughtful people of our time who are concerned about themselves and others are seeking to find the key to understanding. The whole question of relationship is very much a live issue in this search. In reading Brenner's *Elementary Textbook of Psychoanalysis* I was introduced to the word "cathexis," which describes a mental process involving concentration of psychic energy upon the self, another person, a fantasy, an idea, or an object. I am not sure that I fully understand this theory, but it seems to me to be only another way of describing the problem of images and essences. My personal psychology is a collection of cathetects or relationships in which I have participated all my life long. My understanding of other people, my loves and my hates, all my fears and longings are part of my emotional heredity. And this heredity colors my range of relationships to other human beings and to God.

During a weekend conference I heard a speaker equate his feelings for his father with those that he had for God. I began thinking about my relationship with my father and the qualities which I ascribed to God. I felt that God cared for me, that He wanted the best for me. I was His child and He would never disown me. It was hard for me to believe in a stern, forbidding God. In short, I thought about Him in much the same way as I thought of my own father, with whom I had enjoyed a close, warm relationship in which I was treated as a person of great value.

After checking out my own reactions to this idea about God and my father, I asked some others who were at the conference what they thought of it. One young man said that he felt vaguely uneasy, thinking about God; he admitted that during his childhood he had felt that his father was somehow disappointed in him in spite of his efforts to please. An older woman broke down in tears as she related that she had never known her father; she had grown up in an orphanage. It was interesting to see some of the parallels that emerged. Though we didn't try to stretch our comparisons, I think that each of us became aware that the child lingers on in the adult. There seems to be an emotional as well as a rational dimension to the understanding of God's grace.

This conclusion pointed up for me a real problem that Christians must deal with. Somehow, I think we have gotten the idea that because we know the marvelous grace of God and the wonderful life of fellowship with Chirst that we ought not have problems, particularly emotional ones. To admit to difficulties in relationships is evidence of lack of faith in some Christian circles. But in truth, Christians are not exempt from psychological laws any more than they are exempt from, say, the law of gravity. The person who is "hung-up" psychologically before accepting Christ will be hung-up afterwards as well, but the difference is that as a Christian he will have hope and the amazing power of the Holy Spirit at work in his situation. And as he lets God show him the nature of his problems, as he becomes willing to change, as he surrenders himself to the healing that God provides through fellowship with other

54

Christians, then he will begin to enjoy a peace and emotional health that were never possible for him before.

Because I have been in emotional difficulties myself, I have great sympathy for those who have to struggle to find stability in the midst of the complexities of their lives. As a result, I have found myself involved in the past five years with all sorts of people who are trying to find out what it is that makes life worth living. It is no easy job to communicate the reality of God as I know Him in Jesus Christ; many Christians must share my frustrations with the blocks and misunderstandings that arise. I'm afraid that one of my problems in effective communication is that I try to take a shortcut in explaining what commitment to Christ is all about. I must learn to take a person at *his* point of need and to move with him, taking the time to seek the image which expresses the essence of God to him.

Many people have been exposed to the right words for a long time, so long in fact that these words no longer have much meaning. Jane was a good example of a lifetime church member who gave assent to the propositions of Christianity. She was a bright, go-getter type whose main problem was that her husband no longer understood her and her children made her very nervous. The first time we met for lunch (a mutual friend had arranged our meeting) she seemed a dynamo of frustrated energy. Her hands moved constantly, pulling at the tablecloth, rearranging silverware, lighting a fresh cigarette as she snuffed out the old one. We both felt awkward; we weren't quite sure what we should say to each other.

I sent up a prayer for help, took a deep breath, and

began to share with her my experience with the Christ who had made a real difference in the way I lived my life. Rather to my surprise she responded positively. Yes, she believed that Jesus was who He said He was; yes, she had committed her life to Christ. But she was disappointed with the results of commitment, for if anything, her situation was worse than before. I didn't know what to say to her. I had expected arguments, questions—anything but agreement! We concurred on all our theological conclusions, but when she went away from our meeting she was still in the same state of mind she had been when she came. I thought, "What should I have said? She knows all the right words but there's no music." I knew that somehow I must have failed to hear what she was really saying to me. I hoped that she would give me another opportunity to talk with her, but it was many months before I heard from her again. Then she called to invite me to lunch.

The moment I saw her I sensed a change in her, for though she was bubbling over with excitement, the frantic quality was gone. During the summer, she told me, she had met a very wise Christian woman at a place where they had both been vacationing. They had had an opportunity to talk, and Jane had found herself pouring out her terrible feelings of unworthiness, her sense of failure as a human being. These were the feelings that had driven her constantly to prove her value; these were the blocks that had kept her from accepting the image of a forgiving, loving God. How could God ever forgive her, much less love her? But when she found that Gert Behanna could love her and accept her, even though Jane unloaded all her problems on her, then suddenly she could believe that perhaps God *could* love her, too. And the Christian words that she had repeated all her life came alive with meaning.

Perhaps, then, the concept of Christ that is most vital for our fragmented world is the image of Him as the One who reconciles—man to man, man to himself, man to God. He is the Healer. He is the One who tells us who we are, what our own nature is like. He tells us who God is. Christ is the very definition of existence, the only answer to the great question of life itself. "All things were made through him, and without him was not anything made that was made" (John 1:3). As we search for meaning, perhaps the Body of Christ must offer, not a different Christ, but an image with which the people of the world can identify.

Part
Two

THE SEASON
OF SHADOW

Decreed by natural law
The oak must shed its leaves.
Is it less a tree
In winter than in spring?

IF . . .
THE HESITATION OF FAITH

"In its fullest and truest sense faith is an act or attitude of the whole of our inner nature in relation to some other person, whether divine or human."

W. H. GRIFFITH THOMAS, D.D.
in *The Catholic Faith*

Faith is a very personal matter, for although God is and was and ever shall be, each believer must discover this fact for himself. My Christian faith exists because I put my trust in Jesus Christ, Whom I acknowledge to be Deity. As a Christian who is still a human being I am acquainted with doubt, that insidious snake in my private garden. And my doubt, an insult to God to be sure, is a blight and curse upon my very life.

I know a fine woman, of many real virtues, who does a great deal for other people every day of her life. She seeks to make others happy or at least comfortable, but unfortunately she herself finds little joy in what she does. She is a worrier who is mildly uphappy most of the time. As a Christian she is beset by many doubts. She isn't very sure

63

of eternal life but she hopes that it is true. She feels that perhaps it depends on her state of grace at the time of her death. She has difficulty with the sin-bearing nature of Christ's death on the Cross because she doesn't feel that anyone ought to pay for her sins except herself. Her good works abound, but she wonders what she really believes about Jesus. In short, she wants to earn her salvation. Her pride will not allow her to accept such a gift as the love offered freely to mankind by Christ on His Cross. As long as she wonders about the validity of such a salvation, she doesn't have to accept it—or reject it. Her doubt expresses her rebellion against God's plan for the salvation of mankind.

There is the same quality of rebellion in each of us; it echoes in the excuses that we use every day.

"Why me?"

"It wasn't my fault."

"I didn't do it!"

"That's my right!"

"That's not the way *we* do it."

Our defensiveness is, in a way, a pulling back from a position of faith; it is declining to believe what God can do. The old kind of life may be a bit tarnished, but it is at least familiar, its challenges limited. And so it is, I think, that Christians do not so much doubt the existence of God, but rather the extent to which He is able to make us more than we ever could be, were we not involved in a relationship with Him.

I have been a member of the Episcopal church since I was a child, and I have long loved the beauty and the dignity of the worship services, the magnificent words of the liturgy, and the familiar patterns of the ritual. The service of Holy Communion is much the same in the soaring height of a San Francisco cathedral as it is in an open-air chapel at Waring, Texas. The stability of the service lies partly in the fact that the words are the same everywhere and that the minister is a priest, a symbolic office which does not depend on personality. But as much as I love the ritual, I am aware that I can use it as an anesthetic for doubt. Words often repeated do not have to be pondered. As Tennyson says in his poem, "There lives more faith in honest doubt, Believe me, than in half the creeds."

Doubt comes to every Christian—every honest one—for it is difficult to maintain total allegiance to a God unseen. Perhaps this is the reason some search so diligently for an "experience," something tangible such as speaking in tongues, miraculous cures, or visions, or whatever. The long, hard life of faith demands of the Christian an extraordinary amount of courage to enable him to continue to swim against the tide of events toward that unprovable goal, a life with God forever. It is no wonder that we become weary at times and need reassurance that we are headed in the right direction. And in the moment of hesitation, doubt rushes in.

Belief is a powerful force in the life of the human being. It is the leverage that makes possible many things. The whole cult of voodoo rests on the assumption of primitive people that certain persons have extraordinary powers, even to the point of life and death over others. A native, believing that he is under a spell of death, will often weaken and die, for no reason other than that he believes death to be his fate. And lest we scoff at ignorant people, what of the placebos that doctors sometimes use in their treatment? A patient will often get well on sugar pills rather than medication if he believes he is getting medicine. Again and again in His healing ministry Christ equated belief with cure. "And behold, a woman who had suffered from a hemorrhage for twelve years came up behind him and touched the fringe of his garment; for she said to herself, 'If I only touch his garment, I shall be made well.' Jesus turned, and seeing her he said, 'Take heart, daughter; your faith has made you well.' And instantly the woman was made well" (Matthew 9:20-22).

The woman did not cure herself; Christ, in Whom she placed her trust, had the healing power. The terrible effect of doubt is that it cuts us off from the source of our well-being. God loves us, and He would heal us and guide us and comfort us, but He cannot do so unless we trust Him. The curious thing is that we cling to our doubt at times, hugging it to us, choosing to remain estranged and unhappy.

Several years ago my husband and I met regularly with a group of couples who were interested in learning more about themselves and their relationships with each other and with God. It was a free-wheeling group, and we had some great discussions. But there was one man who bothered us all. He hated the Church—his own, specifically, and the Church universal as well. He thought Christ was a thoroughly fascinating, original human being. It was just all those Christians "playing church" that he couldn't stand. There are many who share his feeling, but his wife, a devoted member of their church, was acutely embarrassed by it. She gave time and money and love to further the work of the church, and she was puzzled by her husband's hostility toward something which meant so much to her. One night he started in on "all those hypocrites in the Church," and as he got more and more worked up about his subject, he began to shake with rage. The depth of his hostility revealed the seriousness of his problem. We all tried to help him sort out what was bothering him, but none of us really possessed the skill necessary to reach him.

I have since tried to think through the nature of his problem, even though my opportunity to help has passed. It seems obvious to me that the man's hostility toward the Church was a cover for anger that he felt toward his wife, but which he would not express. But if he wouldn't quarrel with her openly, he certainly saw to it that she was uncomfortable. She never knew quite how to react to his obsession. I think his hostility went beyond that, though. He could not bear for anyone in the group to probe around in the area of his belief about God, although this was one of the reasons we had all agreed to meet together.

On one occasion he took violent exception to my statement that I personally accepted the authority of Scripture. He not only didn't accept the authority of Scripture—he didn't accept *my* acceptance of it. He rejected me on the spot, saying that no intelligent person in the twentieth century could believe that the Bible was anything more than a collection of myths and folk tales.

His reaction was all out of proportion to the issue, a

67

real clue that the root of his problem might be not the Church, but his relationship to God. He never attacked God directly; rather he aimed his hostility toward the Church, or the Bible, or Christians in general. I suspect he was an independent soul who refused to surrender his autonomy to God or man. To rebel against God is a fearful thing. It is safer, if not as polite, to fault the work of the Church and its members. In a verbal exchange he let slip the fact that he didn't trust people. I think it went further than that. He doubted the trustworthiness of God.

It is often hard for me to believe how much God really does love me. I am acutely aware that I don't deserve His love. There are times when it is easy for me to doubt that He has my very best interest in mind as He guides my life. The Bible, though, is full of affirmations to me that He wants me to be happy, to blossom into a personal maturity with the freshness of eternity about it. I hesitate; I hang back from what I know He would have me do; I am afraid to put my whole trust in Him. And, really, He asks so little of me. " 'For truly, I say to you, if you have faith as a grain of mustard seed, you will say to this mountain, "Move hence to yonder place," and it will move; and nothing will be impossible to you' " (Matthew 17:20).

Do I really dare believe Him?

OH, YE ANXIOUS
ONES!

"Anxiety develops automatically whenever the psyche *is overwhelmed by an influx of stimuli too great to be mastered or discharged."*

CHARLES BRENNER, M.D.

"Therefore do not be anxious about tomorrow, for tomorrow will be anxious for itself. Let the day's own trouble be sufficient for the day."

MATTHEW 6:34

DOUBT COMES IN, FOLLOWED CLOSELY BY anxiety. For as faith diminishes, values shift, and suddenly the world inside becomes a strange place. Psychology is very much concerned with anxiety, its causes and effects. Although I could not hope to deal with the many ways to define it scientifically, I can do so in terms of my own experience. For me, anxiety is a state of painful uneasiness, of expectancy of evil or danger without adequate reason. It is the butterflies in my stomach when I have searched the neighborhood and cannot find my small child. It is the nearer side of panic.

All of us are acquainted with such feelings. To a greater or lesser degree we recognize that nameless dread that floats around inside us until it finds a place to focus. But

71

anxiety is by no means the same emotion as fear, although the two are related. Fear is a very necessary human emotion, for it keeps us out of harmful situations. I want my small daughter to fear automobiles, because they can be a menace to her as she crosses the street to play with her friends. Fear is the reasonable expectation of something fairly predictable, such as what an automobile can do if it hits a child. But I don't want my daughter to be so afraid of cars that she runs and hides when she sees one coming.

Anxiety, then, is an unreasonable emotion, based on apprehension of something very remote or unlikely. Anxiety can be produced by doubt, for when a doubt proves to be accurate, then it can be taken as proof of the *possibility*, at least, that all other doubts are valid. And doubt, continued as an attitude, becomes pessimism. I am acquainted with a woman who worries quite earnestly about atomic wars, national economic disasters, catastrophes of wind and weather, none of which she can do much about. She wakes in the middle of the night to ponder the possibilities of a race riot in our city. Her conversation is slanted toward her conviction that things will most surely get worse. And, in a way, she's right; we live in perilous times. But her attitude is hard to take seriously, except for the fact that she really suffers from her anxieties. Perhaps her particular anxieties have an environmental origin —she probably grew up with anxious parents who impressed her early with the dangers of living.

The world can be a puzzling experience for those strangers, our children, who must live in the dimensions of an adult world. Strong self-centeredness is nature's protection for small people who find doorknobs out of reach. The back yard stretches to the edge of their world, and time seems to stand still when you cannot divide it into minutes. "Just a moment, darling" may sound like *never* to a child. And warnings are posted everywhere: "Watch out, don't fall!" "You'll have a stomach ache if you eat any more ice cream." "Brush your teeth, or you'll get a cavity."

The child is smart enough to realize that the world can be a dangerous place. At the same time, he has to try things in order to grow. To further his problem, he may be urged to mask his natural fears. How many times do parents say things like "There's nothing to be afraid of in the dark," or, "Now stop that crying! You know mother's not going to be gone long." And, "Susie didn't *mean* to throw sand in your face. We don't want her to feel bad, so tell her it's all right." Bombarded by directions and impressions, both negative and positive, the child soon confuses danger and discomfort with the dread of them. The pattern of anxiety is established.

Few of us are lucky enough to grow up free of anxiety, but recognizing that one is anxious is the first step toward being freed of the bonds of apprehension. I have examined the real nature of anxiety as I have faced my acute difficulty with flying in airplanes. For a long time I had concluded that I suffered from an inner ear disturbance, for when I traveled by air, the plane no sooner left the ground than I was nauseated. And I stayed that way until I got back down to earth! Wryly, I claimed that I was living in the wrong century, for I was sure that I'd have been much happier traveling in a covered wagon. But, alas, I do live in the jet age and in order to get anywhere with reasonable ease, I must fly. Not only that, my husband thinks flying is fun, so he took the necessary training to get his pilot's license and then bought an airplane. While it is convenient to be able to go places and do things in your own plane, it was discouraging to me to have to count on being sick each and every time, regardless of weather.

It was at this same period in my life that I was involved in the fascinating—and painful—process of consultation with a psychiatrist. During one session, I half-jokingly asked him what I could do about motion sickness, since it had become obvious that I'd be flying a good bit. He shot back at me the question, "You mean, e-motion sickness?" I was insulted by his lack of sympathy and by the insinuation that my emotions were playing such tricks on me. I dropped the subject and decided to rely on Dramamine.

During the past five years Bob and I have been invited to retreats and conferences as lay witnesses, to tell what Christ really means in our lives. As Christians, we have been grateful for these marvelous opportunities and we have felt that witnessing was something God wanted us to do. Naturally, accepting these invitations has involved more travel by air, and I prayed most earnestly that I could learn to be comfortable flying. (I spent much of the time in flight remembering all the Scripture I knew by heart.) But I still had my same old problem, except that now I could no longer use Dramamine because it made me too sleepy to be able to speak effectively.

Then, I decided to consider seriously the suggestion that the psychiatrist had made earlier. Perhaps my problem *was* emotion sickness, and the emotion might be anxiety, although in all the thousands of miles I had flown I had never been in what I could call a dangerous situation. My reaction to flying could not rightly be called fear. I was conscious of the statistics that prove the relative safety of air travel; still, I must be anxious about flying. I tried to pinpoint the sources of my anxiety. As the mother of three children I feared that I might not live to see them grown, that I would leave them orphans, to their everlasting emotional disability. It would be worse if Bob and I were killed together. That's a reasonable fear, but it applies to automobile travel as well; cars are more dangerous than planes. Disaster is a part of life; a person cannot guarantee the length of his life, no matter how careful he is. And besides, this process of reasoning failed to explain why I had been affected by planes this way since I was eight.

I thought back to my first flight. During World War II my father had gone back to the University of Texas in order to get another degree. He wanted to be accepted by the Army Corps of Engineers, but he was past the age limit except for specialized jobs. Because my parents' plans were unsettled, I was to live with my aunt and attend a very fine private school at which she was a teacher. I flew from Corpus Christi to Nashville by myself, under care of the stewardess. I don't remember feeling frightened during that flight; I do remember being sick at my stomach.

Looking back, I can guess what was really going on in

75

SEASONS OF THE SOUL

that eight-year-old girl. I was going toward a new place
to live, with a different situation in school. I was leaving
behind the security of parents and home and playmates.
That airplane must have become the focus of all my ap-
prehensions and fears, and so it has remained all these
years. Each time I board a plane my fears are replayed
in my unconscious; I'm grown now, but the feelings linger
on. When I finally realized something of the basis of the
feelings involved, I began to be able to name my fears. I
could refute the old ones which no longer had meaning in
my present situation. I still have some bad moments in
flight, but my panic is no longer blind. And sometimes, I
can actually enjoy the miracle of the jet age!

As a Christian, I had been terribly ashamed of my
problem about flying because it seemed to be a lack of
faith in God on my part. It was as though I doubted that
God had my best interest at heart, but until I found the
source of the fear behind the doubt, I could not be set free.
Perhaps we need to acknowledge our actual feelings and
to understand that emotions cannot be imposed on us by
other people or by a situation, except as we give permission. So maybe the solution to anxieties is to look within
ourselves to find the answers God would give us. God didn't
give me instant peace about flying, even in response to my
fervent prayer. He gave me something much better—an
understanding of myself that set me free.

A SLIPPERY PATH
IN THE WAY OF DARKNESS

Foul bird that sits above
My weary road
And waits,
To rip and tear
The clothes, the flesh,
The very heart from soul.

Dark is his name
And fearsome;
His shadow will not depart from me
Though swift I run.
And yet—
In light there is no dark,
What shall I fear?

Except the light
I cannot live.

The heart knows its own bitterness and no stranger shares its joy.

PROVERBS 14:10

THE DAY IS SUNNY, THE AIR CLEAR AND COOL from a recent rain. It would be a lovely day to spend out of doors. But instead I stare out the window, reflecting bitterly that the contrast between what I see and what I feel is all the more a bad joke. Inside me the clouds are thick, obscuring the sun. Depression has moved in on my soul with the cold softness of fog.

It is hard for me to know what has caused this abrupt swing downward in my mood. Perhaps I cannot postpone my disillusionment any longer. I feel overwhelmed by deceptive love or shattered images or the failure of friendship. Or maybe I am discouraged—the days come and go so fast and I'm haunted by what I'm not doing. My life will be over before I have done all the things I want to do

79

so much. It could be the depression of doubt. This day I feel not at all like a radiant Christian, but rather a reclusive creature who is skeptical, bored, disappointed. I'm like the house Christ described—all cleaned out, but occupied by demons worse than before.

Everyone suffers at some time a depression, mild or otherwise. Everyone has some stress level, beyond which he has had enough, emotionally. Usually a person can rise to heights of heroism in a crisis which calls forth his best effort. A fall on a snowy slope, a fractured leg—the pain blurs with the determination to bear it with courage. But then comes the long convalescence, the hobbling around, the irritation of physical limitation and boredom. This is when depression can set in. Fortunately, in this form, it is self-limiting. With the removal of the cast, spirits rise.

For some of us, though, depression is a recurring problem. I know a good bit about it from actual experience; I have always been subject to mood swings, extreme in their intensity and variety. For a time I could wake each morning and decide immediately whether it felt like a good day or a bad one. As I decided, so the day became. My pattern of depression was often self-perpetuating, so that some event or person had to intervene before the fog lifted.

There are legitimate physical problems which induce a feeling of mild depression. The "low" feeling that goes with a head cold is a typical example with which we are all familiar. With recovery from the cold the depression vanishes. It is impossible to separate body and soul. An interesting question, though, is whether the cold causes the depression or the depression causes the cold?

More seriously, depression which lengthens into a continuing state of mind can be as dangerous as untreated cancer. People die of depression. Suicide now ranks among the ten leading causes of death in the United States. Research by psychologists and psychiatrists indicates that actual chemical changes occur in persons who are losing their psychological defenses against self-destruction.[1] On the brighter side, a new drug, lithium carbonate, promises a simple chemical means of lessening the impact of depression. But a person caught in the downward spiral of depression should get medical help immediately.

The kind of depression I have had to deal with in my own experience has its origin in frustration, when things aren't going the way I want them to, when my desires have been repeatedly denied. If anxiety nibbles at one's confidence, depression admits to failure.

The persons most susceptible to depression are those who doubt their own worth. They mistrust their ability to cope with life. They feel oppressed by others, by fate. Self-pity creeps in to accentuate the process. They have acquired unrealistic standards and so are forever falling short of the mark. Depression is their psychological surrender in response to failure, and the amount of emotional energy expended to keep depression from becoming despair is tremendous. Often there is little left to invest in love or joy or pleasure.

Sometimes the inevitable march of the years lessens

1. Jane E. Brody, "Psychologist Says More Care Could Reduce Suicide Cases," *New York Times*, March 30, 1969.

one's sense of values. Most of us find our hope in goals, or dreams at least, and our plans for the future urge us to do what is necessary today. As long as we are able to look ahead to something meaningful, we feel that the effort of living is worth the reward. But there comes a time when we realize that many dreams must be put away; the attendant sadness may bring paralysis of action.

Then, too, aging usually brings health problems. It's hard not to be depressed when one doesn't feel good. For a man, retirement often means an end to the joy of productive effort. All the golf or fishing in the world can't fill the void that he feels. An older woman may suddenly realize that though she feels thirty inside, she looks twice that old. And perhaps she isn't needed as she was before the children flew the nest. In later years there seems to be an abundance of time to dwell on fears and phobias and useless regrets.

But does a person *have* to sink into the hollow of depression? I have decided that I don't want to waste time being depressed, so I've tried to analyze my susceptibility to it. And I have come to recognize the series of small steps, each one taken consecutively, which lead me into a state of depression. The pattern is reasonably the same in every case:

1. I experience a defeat or loss of some kind. It is often a disappointment of expectation.

2. I begin to dwell on all the aspects of the disappointment, examining minutely the details and the *feelings* that the occasion prompts.

3. I become subjective and begin to try to see what

shortcomings of my own are responsible for the outcome.

4. I conclude that to lose a battle is to concede the war.

5. I give myself up to gloom.

Recognizing that process gives me the option to choose my actions, for I have learned that it is possible to decline to enter into the state of depression, if one so chooses. The pattern can be altered:

1. I experience a defeat or loss of some kind. It is often a disappointment of expectation.

2. I try to be realistic about the situation. I acknowledge that in the normal course of life I will have my percentages of hits and misses. But I have learned from playing tennis that the surest way to lose a game is to dwell on that last bad shot.

3. I refuse to seek out faults that may not be there. I often deny these self-destructive thoughts in the name of Christ, for whoever said that "discouragement is of the devil" certainly knew what he was talking about.

4. I resolve to try to handle the situation differently in the future, if possible, so that the outcome may be more positive. Repeated failures trigger most depressions.

5. I move on mentally and physically to something else. Action is a good antidote for introspection.

I have learned to handle some of these oppressive moods of mine. If I have an argument with my husband and I say some things I wish I hadn't said, I don't have to add the agony of depression and brooding to the burden of being wrong. I can face up to being less than even-tempered, and apologize, and plan to react differently next time. If death intrudes on my life and my loss is very real, I can grieve openly and seek to incorporate into my own life the best of what that loved and lost one gave to me. Grief can be a means of expanding the dimensions of understanding. If I am lonely and my very existence seems to be unimportant in the scheme of things, I reflect on the absolute uniqueness of my creation and on the love of my Creator. And if the time comes when it is really dark inside, from the depths of the hell I have made for myself I cry to God, "Help me. I cannot free myself!" And the healing light of God pours through my darkened soul and the weight of despair lifts. The crisis is over, for the moment.

THE FIRE
INSIDE

. . . an orb of resentment
dipped in the silver vat of hate;
A small, hard pellet,
Undissolved.

Can a man carry fire in his bosom
and his clothes not be burned?
Or can one walk on hot coals
and his feet not be scorched?

PROVERBS 6:27–28

BEING WITH SOME PEOPLE IS LIKE WALKING barefoot through a field of glass—the only question is how badly you are going to get cut up before you get through. Most of us at some time or other have been on the receiving end of emotional mayhem—the victims of obvious or subtle hostility.

I have spent a great deal of time and effort during my life in pursuit of favorable opinions from the people I know. I suppose I have always been a bit sensitive, and particularly to disapproval from just about anybody. It always comes as a shock to me when someone doesn't like me. It hurts.

As a Christian, I have tried to learn to be objective about hostility toward me as a person. In doing so I hope I have learned something about the withering, killing unlove which plagues people and communities and nations. I know I have come to recognize the real basis of my own resentments toward others and to look for honest causes for dislike.

It is my guess that the emotion which prompts my hostility is fear of the power that another person has over the course of my life. If the fear grows, I react with the desire not only to protect myself but to strike back, hard. The suspicion that a woman is trying to damage my reputation by saying nasty things behind my back encourages me to bring forth my own arsenal of gossip about *her*. If I find myself confronted by her in person, I can choose to be cool but polite, assuming a neutral position. Or I can launch the attack and accuse her head-on of being a terrible gossip. A defensive reaction would lead me to avoid any exchange at all with her, out of fear of further attack.

When nations indulge in the same sort of antipathy, it may mean a cold war, a hot conflict, or an uneasy peace. France and Germany, for example, have contended over Alsace-Lorraine for generations. Though the boundaries may now be legally settled, the mistrust and hostility linger on. Self-interest dictates that we fear what others may do to us. But because open conflict is costly, both to nations and to individuals, we tend to indulge our hostile feelings in more subtle ways.

Sometimes we are hard put to name our fear. The suspicion which exists between black America and white America rests on a number of fears, most of which have been inherited from the past. Ours is a sorry legacy of generations of mistakes and misunderstandings on both sides; until we all lay aside our vague fears, the enmity will continue. The saddest aspect is the waste of emotional energy involved in maintaining hostility.

Have you ever been so mad that your hands were shaking and your knees got weak? Rage prompts a rush of adrenalin, and even after the initial crisis, the burden of anger lingers on. In imaginary conversations, the enemy gets told off; elaborate schemes of revenge are devised; apprehension over possible retaliation builds up. Around some persons the very air becomes laden with the electricity of smouldering anger, undischarged. To spend much time with such individuals is an uncomfortable experience; if hostility is an established behavioral pattern for them, you may be certain that they are looking for an object to strike out at. Hostility cannot be permanently suppressed—this is like trying to hold a beach ball under water; it is always popping up to the surface. And intense hostility toward others usually says more about the hostile person than about the object of resentment.

Hostility is a doubly damning emotion, a real two-edged sword of destruction. As a Christian I must learn to cope with my hostile feelings toward others as well as theirs toward me. Both can damage healthy personality. I need first to recognize the signals of hostility, those I send and those I receive. Some of these signals are familiar— loaded words and phrases, for instance. "Well, I hope it works out all right for you." (But it may not.) "What have you done to yourself? You look wonderful!" (Not like you looked the last time I saw you.) "He seems capable, but . . ." (He really probably isn't.) The uneasiness we feel in the face of these apparently innocent remarks is our response to what we sense is really being said.

Another clue to what is really going on inside a person is over-reaction, that is, an emotional reaction out of all proportion to the situation. During a small group meeting when I referred to God as my heavenly Father, I was bitterly challenged by a woman who violently disagreed with me. The more she talked about what a mistake it was to look upon God this way, the more upset she became. God was our Judge, not a forgiving Father. It was obvious I had, with my remark, cut close to some real problem that she had. Actually, her hostility toward me had just leaked out of a larger pool of uncertainty. Some people simply act out their emotions. Murders are committed for a variety of reasons, but one of the most common is the boiling over of fear and hate. The corrosiveness of hostility finally destroys both victim and assassin.

Most of us handle our negative feelings in less violent ways. I do know, though, that if I choose to harbor a resentment, I will lose no opportunity to reinforce it, simply to prove that I was justified in my initial hurt. I am particularly vulnerable when my pride is involved.

Soon after the publication of *The Real and Only Life,* I gave a copy to a couple whose judgment I valued, although we sometimes had theological differences of opinion. I was eager to have their verdict. Two weeks passed with no word from them. I decided that they were embarrassed to tell me what they really thought. Then, I saw the husband at a shopping center. We visited very casually for a few moments and then said goodbye. As he was walking away, he suddenly turned and said, "I meant to tell you how much I enjoyed your book. It's really good!" He sounded sincere, but I mumbled my thanks and hurried on. Didn't he understand what that book meant to me? It was a part of *me*, exposed to acceptance or rejection. How could he be so casual?

The more I thought about it, the more I resented him. By the time I got home I was really mad. I poured out my hostility to my husband; he surprised me by his lack of sympathy. He pointed out that our friends were interested and involved in a great many things beside my book. Perhaps I had blown up their response to it all out of proportion. It was hard for me to accept this, for I had been hurt and I was ready to write them off as friends. But I could also see the truth in what Bob said. My anticipation had set up unrealistic expectations; I had also wanted to prove something to these people. As rationality prevailed, I offered up to God in prayer the hostility I felt toward these friends who had disappointed me. I'm not sure even now that I am completely free of my resentment, but it is my conscious choice not to hold it against them.

One of the hardest lessons I have to learn is that I cannot indulge in resentment or dreams of getting even. Something curdles inside me when I linger over hates, wrongs, injustices, wounds. Because I am human I do feel these barbs, and very keenly. I have to offer up the hurts to God, knowing that of myself I am not big enough to really forgive. But neither am I strong enough to carry resentments around, for the weight of them can overwhelm me.

In the Sermon on the Mount, Christ speaks of turning the other cheek when a person strikes you. If this statement is taken at face value it sounds weak, even ridiculous. How could it possibly do you or the other person any good if he hits you again? But if Christ is talking about the attitude that a Christian is to have toward those who wrong him, then this is something else. I think Christ knew the consequences to a person's soul of hostility, of striking back, of plotting revenge. He is saying, "Don't do violence to yourself by hating the man who has hurt you. Better that you let him hit you again than to freeze into hate."

There is always a balance, a justice in the words of the Scriptures. In the same passage Jesus makes a curious statement about the peril of giving dogs things that are holy, and about casting pearls before swine (Matthew 7:6). It seems clear warning that what we hold dear and special may be garbage to someone else. It is foolish to continue to beat one's heart against another's stone wall, in the hope of establishing a good relationship. Sometimes with the best will in the world one cannot have it, if the other person does not respond to the offer of concern. Songs about unrequited love testify to that. It takes two responsive human beings to have a satisfactory relationship.

To ask why a relationship is bad is often useless. I have spent much valuable time and a lot of psychic energy trying to understand the motives and reactions of people with whom I don't get along. Often I have to conclude that even if I did understand them better, I still wouldn't enjoy being in their company. The great variety of experiences open to all of us is insurance that each of us will be different in thought patterns, emotional responses, and background. Some of us have such diverse ways of looking at life that we will never understand each other. (I am sure that most men feel this way about all women!) It is healthy to respect differences and wise to know what cannot be. In my own life, to my real regret, there have been several individual "moments of awakening" marked by the realization that a meaningful relationship could not exist with a certain individual, at least not on my terms. I cannot force another to trust me, to care for me, to wish for me the very best. Sometimes the barriers of envy, misunderstanding, or unhappiness are too high to leap over.

Nevertheless, if I am to mature into the kind of loving person Christ wants me to be, I must face up to my cross-grained relationships and my hostilities. I can at least look at them with as much honesty as I can muster. I can check my reactions with others who may be more objective than I. (Is it me or thee?) I can recognize what triggers my negative feelings, the words and actions which repeatedly provoke me. If I decide I am at fault, I have the option to ask God to help me change. But if I am the victim of someone else's hang-up, then I can try to understand and at least give him the benefit of putting his words and actions toward me in the best possible light. And failing all else, I can accept the fact that for reasons beyond my control the relationship is a poor one and it is best for me to commit that relationship to God. " 'You have heard that it was said, "You shall love your neighbor and hate your enemy." But I say to you, Love your enemies and pray for them who persecute you, so that you may be sons of your Father who is in heaven; for he makes his sun rise on the evil and on the good, and sends rain on the just and on the unjust' " (Matthew 5:43-44).

A MEASURE
OF GUILT

". . . Let me alone, for my days are a breath.
What is man, that thou dost make so much of him,
*   and that thou dost set thy mind on him,*
dost visit him every morning,
*   and test him every moment?"*

JOB 7:16–18

". . . Know then that God exacts of you
less than your guilt deserves."

JOB 11:6

IN ALL THE WORLD THERE IS NO CREATURE
except man who suffers from the exquisite
pain of moral responsibility. Some animals of the higher
orders approximate such discernment, but even the most
intelligent beast is not held responsible if his conduct results in injury to another. The lion is not judged guilty
for the death of his lunch, a hapless wildebeest! Genesis
describes man's uniqueness in comparison to the rest of
God's creation by speaking in terms of original innocence
and the loss of it in tasting of the fruit of the tree of
knowledge of good and evil. Alas for mankind! There can
be no return to innocence, for each human being senses
that there is right and there is wrong. One of the legal tests
for responsibility, for judgment of sanity, is the ability to

distinguish between right and wrong. To lack such comprehension is to be classified as something less than fully human.

Assuming then that there are standards of right and wrong, what are they and how are they arrived at? Certainly the culture in which an individual grows and learns imposes many collective ideals. The wide differences in cultures only serve to point up the fact that though the standards differ radically according to time and place, all societies have some yardstick by which to judge behavior. Acceptance of the standard involves personal identification with it by the individual. My five-year-old daughter practices being grown-up by answering the telephone and imitating what she has heard me say. She uses the phrase "just a moment, please," not because she is intent on being polite, but because she has heard "big people" say it that way.

As each of us grows from infancy into the middle years of childhood, we acquire in the process a conscience, what Freud called a superego. This superego begins to give us internal standards; it makes us function as moral beings in a physical world which seems indifferent to moral choice. Biblical writers seek to express this problem; indeed the book of Job deals with the dilemma of a man who has tried to be good and found only grief and pain as his reward. No, the observance of moral standards does not insure tranquillity in this world; as the book of Matthew states, rain is no respecter of persons; and neither is sorrow nor illness nor pain nor death.

The question of Job's guilt arises from his attempt to

explain his misfortune. Surely some omission, some hidden fault is the reason that God has withdrawn His favor. Job and his friends search his life, but the poor man doesn't know what it is that he is guilty of. He has tried to measure up in every way. For much of his lifetime, his virtue has seemingly been rewarded with success and happiness, and then the roof caves in on him. He loses family, possessions, even his health. All of us sympathize with Job, although we may not have experienced his extreme circumstance; surely each of us must conclude, as Job did, "I can't avoid the truth. I *am* guilty. And I hope that I don't have to pay the full price of what I know I have done wrong."

It seems that the standards for man are impossibly high. Some seek to make their peace with standards by living according to ethical principles which are comfortable. If they are uneasy, they conclude that perhaps they need to lower their sights a bit. The so-called New Morality reflects this attitude. If people can't live up to present standards, we'll just tailor them to what people can manage.

On the other side are those whose standards are nothing less than absolute perfection, all day, every day. The Jewish faith, based as it is on observance of rules and regulations, puts an overwhelming burden on its members. To keep the whole Law is impossible. At the time of Jesus' life on earth, a particular religious class, the Pharisees, felt that they had come the closest of anybody to the meticulous observance of the finer points of the Law. Jesus said to them, "But woe to you, scribes and Pharisees, hypocrites! because you shut the kingdom of heaven against men; for you neither enter yourselves, nor allow those who would enter to go in" (Matthew 23:13–14).

A little further on in the passage he continues, "Woe to you, scribes and Pharisees, hypocrites! for you are like whitewashed tombs, which outwardly appear beautiful, but within they are full of dead men's bones and all uncleanness. So you also outwardly appear righteous to men, but within you are full of hypocrisy and iniquity" (Matthew 23:27–28). If there was ever warning against the striving for worldly perfection, we find it in this pointed passage. Surely even the most passionate seeker after righteousness acknowledges, deep inside his own heart, that his outward conduct and inward spirit often don't match. Each of us is imperfect and it is our imperfection which separates us from perfect God.

Well, what do you do with guilt, once you have acknowledged it? Can you give it away, mail it to a friend, seek absolution, bury it inside? Guilt has a way of sticking to us. We may try to project it—"*I* didn't do it. He did!" We may deny it—"I certainly can't be expected to worry about that." Or we may simply try to beg off—"Everyone drives too fast. It's our way of life." But guilt is like pain; it is a warning to our souls that something is wrong. A person who lacks the physical sensation of pain is forever burning his fingers, bruising his shins and otherwise getting into dangerous situations because he lacks the signal of pain. So it is with guilt, the inescapable sign of the discrepancy between what we are to be and what we are now. Guilt can be the guide to our potential; to seek to avoid knowledge of it is to avoid emotional maturity. But let me add quickly, guilt and condemnation are different, for condemnation is a word without hope, but guilt offers the possibility of repentance.

Nevertheless, guilt is one of the emotions from which people try to escape. They use alcohol, heroin, tranquilizers, compulsive involvement in work, and even religious conformity, to quiet the accuser inside. Does the alcoholic perhaps drink a second drink to quiet his guilty feeling over the first one? Does the church worker who neglects her family in order to spend night and day at the church wish to have an answer to her accuser inside? "You're guilty. Shame! Shame! You're guilty!" The voice echoes inside although we try not to hear it. But it is easier by far to deal with the criticism of others than to still the voice of conscience.

Who is the accuser, and who the judge? And the advocate, the lawyer for the defense? And more to the point, since we know our own guilt, how is the penalty to be paid? It is at this point that human resources fail. Psychology seeks to help us alleviate guilt or at least the pain of it. But the psychiatrist is only another fellow human being; he cannot offer pardon, absolution. He can help me rid myself of unearned guilt, of my emotional response to other people's negative attitudes toward me. He can enable me to pinpoint unrealistic expectations which goad me into false guilt. But sooner or later, as I peel back the layers of my own personality, I come to a core which is essentially wrong, somehow. It is this hard heart of tangled self-love which produces my feelings of real guilt. I

101

must answer to the charge of self-centeredness with an emphatic "Yes!" I must honestly admit, "God, it's true. I love others, at times. I try to love You. But, oh, how I do love myself!"

God knows my predicament; His love long ago made provision for my wrongness. One by one my defenses fall and my excuses fail, and I am left with only this plea—I am justified by faith in Christ. I accept Him as my substitute, the One who pays the penalty for me.

I do not fully understand the implications of the Cross of Christ. The Bible tells me that His sacrifice of Himself lets me borrow the righteousness of the one person who ever walked the earth without doing wrong. I cannot, now or ever, claim more for myself than this, that Christ has reconciled me with God. It is a humbling thought for my proud heart, but there it is. I can only gratefully accept what God has done in providing atonement for my very sins.

"For in him all the fulness of God was pleased to dwell, and through him to reconcile to himself all things, whether on earth or in heaven, making peace by the blood of his cross" (Colossians 1:19–20).

Part
Three

THE SEASON
OF LIGHT

May those who sow in tears,
reap with shouts of joy!

PROPHET OR PRAGMATIST?

I will live
And move and be,
In spite of all who pick and pry
And seek to render impotent
That which meaning is for me,

A sacred thing
Man's right to be,
Just as he is;
Not gainsayed, nor compassed round
By sneers and silent laughter.

The mystic child must live alone,
Shut off by what he knows.
Maligned, misunderstood;
But how seek else
When awareness is the blessing
And the curse.

*"And it shall come to pass afterward,
   that I will pour out my spirit on all flesh;
Your sons and your daughters shall prophesy,
   your old men shall dream dreams,
And your young men shall see visions."*

JOEL 2:28

THIS TWENTIETH CENTURY AFTER CHRIST
must surely go down in history as a prag-
matic age. The recent acceleration of scientific knowledge
and application of that knowledge to a way of living stag-
gers the human mind, except that by now we are so accustomed to progress that we take it for granted. We accept
the fact that man will explore the universe; only the details remain to be worked out. Practical wonders and
improbable solutions are the order of the day. We have
come to expect ever-pyramiding technical information and
skill to produce more and more of every modern miracle.
The important question seems to be, "Does it work?"

Yet in the midst of such a blooming of the potential of
the human brain, there is unrest, among individuals and

nations. We are a bit unsure of what the future really holds. Scientific achievement will continue to bring advantages to mankind and the physical conditions of life. Surely people should be getting happier and healthier and wiser and more content as we gain these advantages. But it does not seem to work out this way. We have already discovered that science can be a two-edged sword, capable of setting us free or of piercing us through.

Often from the scientific segment of society comes the urgent warning that all is not well in our materialistic world. Predictions can be gloomy. If an atomic holocaust doesn't destroy us, the population explosion may. Medicine has made the prospect of extended life spans entirely possible through organ transplants. But what of the older people already shoved aside in our youth-oriented culture? And the sharp sight of the youth of today has forced the rest of us to take a look at some things we would rather not see.

Most of us wish a lot of problems would just go away. It would be wonderful if there were no such thing as marijuana. Sometimes I find myself weary of even *hearing* about racial tension, student protest, the war in Vietnam. Most of the books on the best-seller lists seem to consist only of four-letter words. My television set brings me live coverage of assassinations and funerals of state so frequently that the horror is dulled. I abhor the violence of the times and the loss of life, the waste of lives cut off too soon.

But these things are part of what I know as life. I can seek to avoid them, but I know they are there. To fail to recognize evil is in a way to surrender to it. And if we listen to what is being said through all the turmoil, we can hear the voice of prophecy which refuses to be stilled, even in the midst of so much confusion. It seems that now, as always, political, social, and personal unrest is created by the gap between pragmatism and prophecy, between doing and being.

Who are the prophets of the day? The word "prophet" may have for some of us the connotation of a bearded old man in tattered robes who periodically predicts dire happenings. Actually, by definition, a prophet is one who speaks for another, an inspired revealer of the truth. Although we tend to think of this in terms of those men in the Old Testament who spoke for God in their troubled times, I think the deeper meaning of the word includes far more than that.

The modern inheritors of the prophetic tradition include writers, poets, artists—the interpreters of human events. These creative personalities tell the people of our time something about themselves. They are the lonely ones in the crowd, a step ahead of the band to which the rest of us march apace. Some of them live a life which casts a large shadow. The everyday events of living have for them an intensity of experience beyond the usual emotional involvement. They try to paint the dream, to say that for which there are no words, to re-create the rhythm of the heartbeat in the resonance of a guitar. They seek to stretch the fabric of personality in order to understand what man can never fully know. They repeat the age-old question of the meaning of human existence; the answers vary, but never the question. Whether they even know it or not, they are speaking for the rest of us; and beyond that for Another, for all prophecy ultimately makes clear to the people of the time the eternal will of God.

If this culture of our time can be called a pop culture, then we need to listen to its pop prophets. Garish color, frantic music—louder, brighter, more mechanical; depersonalized sex, instant gratification; sick humor; drugs, dreams. Listen to the words (if you can distinguish them) of the songs. True love is still around, but so is loneliness, separation, sadness, the need for identity.

Even the weird looks of some of the popular groups, copied by many of the young, is an expression of revolt against what they call conformity. The sad thing, though, is that they all wind up looking like a type, conforming not to the standards of the square world, but to the code of the bizarre, which becomes merely boring, repeated often enough. If you've seen one hippie, you can recognize another. But the fact that the hippies have attracted so much attention may be proof that they are expressing something valid about man's need to be unique and individual, about his desire to live a fresh life, to be free to become all that he can be. The hippie movement is dying a natural death because it states the problem, but comes up with the wrong answer. Nevertheless, what attracts the young to a group such as the Beatles is their fresh way of saying what must be said about modern patterns of society. Discounting what is gimmicky about their art, we must recognize that they are prophesying for our time.

In quite a different way the artist Andrew Wyeth is saying something in his painting that perhaps makes us uncomfortable. His landscapes are beautiful, detailed studies of an American scene that is fast disappearing under the onslaught of suburbs, highways, industrial complexes, and mechanization of the remaining open land. When he paints people, he records with exactitude the loneliness and isolation and estrangement that man feels today, from the land and from himself. Wyeth paints what he sees with an understated intensity produced by strong feeling held in check by the will. Last year in a museum in Los Angeles I saw a collection of his work. Included in it was a painting called "The Drifter." It was a portrait of a Negro man of about thirty. The power of his shoulders was in sharp contrast with his lowered eyes. What I read in that man's face said far more to me about the alienation of the black people than all the headlines about ghettos in flames. Andrew Wyeth had interpreted for me, in terms of the life of one human being, a social catastrophe of which I am a part.

Now Wyeth may not have set out to do this; he may not even know he has done it. Artists love the art more than what others say about the art, and prophets are often unaware that they are just that. The fact remains that he prophesied for me, telling me something that I needed to feel, rather than know.

The scope of modern Christian prophecy encompasses many different personalities and viewpoints, from Billy Graham to Teilhard de Chardin. Dr. Graham preaches a basic message about sin and salvation, about human lostness and the way to get back home again. It is so simple; surely people would be tired by now of hearing the same

111

thing over and over. But to the contrary—the crowds at his crusades continue to grow and people by the hundreds come forward in response to his appeal for commitment to Christ. More than that, Billy Graham is bold enough to bring the Christian faith into millions of homes in prime time on television.

On the other hand, the Jesuit paleontologist Pierre Teilhard de Chardin has formulated a very complex vision of man and God. The ordinary mind finds his concepts difficult to grasp. I confess that in reading his work I only sometimes *think* I catch a glimpse of what he means by ultimate convergence. But perhaps what I sense most strongly is his prophetic note. In this twentieth century he is trying to tell us a bit more about ourselves and about God. He offers us new clues to the awesome dimensions of the God we so dimly perceive.

Both of these men are following in the tradition of Christian prophecy, speaking for our Lord in the context of the age. Though many voices all around us are raised to tell us what is wrong with our world, few offer any solutions to the problems. It would seem that only those prophecies based on the eternal plan of God stand the test of time.

A long time ago Jesus asked: "What good can it do a man to gain the whole world at the price of his own soul? What can a man offer to buy back his soul once he has lost it?" (Mark 8:36–37, Phillips). In other words, what will it matter if our world becomes technically perfect, if in the process man loses God? I do not believe that there is in the whole world enough material comfort to be found to make up for the loss of a resting place for the soul. Augustine, Bishop of Hippo in the fourth century, expressed this in a beautiful way: "Thou hast created us unto thyself and our hearts find no rest until they rest in thee." The world needs its prophets to point the way back to God, to show us the discrepancy between what we are as men and what we may become as children of God.

If society needs its prophets, this is not to say that it does not need its pragmatists as well. After all, who but the pragmatists makes this present world go round? They are the producers, the organizers, the executors of ideas, the shapers of events. They grow food, clothe people, discover cures for disease, send rockets into space, govern nations. They deliver my milk, write my newspaper, fix my automobile. In terms of the Gospel commandments, pragmatists visit the sick, comfort the widow, stand ready with cups of cool water for tired, dusty wanderers. Christian pragmatists are involved with the "Social Gospel," practicing what James said: "But some one will say, 'You have faith and I have works.' Show me your faith apart from your works, and I by my works will show you my faith" (James 2:18).

God needs not only His prophets but His pragmatists to make this garden of earth flourish, and truly it would seem that each of us is a blend of both. The human personality combines the call to action with the revelation of intuition. A person both feels and acts. Who, though, is pure prophet; and where, short of a computer-robot, can one find a complete pragmatist? It is necessary, however, for us to recognize these two distinct strains, for the vital-

113

ity of human life depends on the interaction between them.

In our family, my husband, Bob, could be classified by profession as a pragmatist—he is a homebuilder. I am a writer, so that puts me in the prophetic class. Certainly a book can do nothing more than communicate, for no one ever ate one, at least with much satisfaction! Bob is orderly as far as his personal possessions are concerned; I get so absorbed in ideas that I don't see the cobwebs in the corners. Ah, but my husband has in the last two years become a painter; he interprets what he sees with paint and paper so that others may see something they have never seen before in quite that way. I do have a house to care for, children to nurture, cooking to do, and those activities certainly fall into the pragmatic category. So it is that my husband and I combine the qualities of pragmatist and prophet, each of us unique in the combination of the two characteristics.

And though each human being is a combination, one trait is usually dominant. This is one way we label people —he's a dreamer, she's a go-getter, he'll never get it off the ground, they can't see the forest for the trees! Even the Christian Church divides itself sometimes, doctrine vs. doing. Prophets and pragmatists seem to stand at opposite sides of experience, eyeing each other coolly, never quite understanding the motivation of the other.

Surely the world needs both, and perhaps for the Christian the Lord Jesus Christ is the perfect blend of both. He came to earth that man might know what God is like; He became flesh, the incarnation of the Word. He interpreted God to the people of His day—indeed, to all people for all time—and on the cross He offered Himself as the only way•of salvation for mankind. He preached the salvation of God and He *was* the salvation of God. We who choose to belong to Him, to speak for Him, to offer ourselves in service to others in His name—perhaps we need to be His pragmatists and His prophets, to let the full impact of our personal and corporate witness say to the world what it is longing to hear and do for the world what must be done.

THE MYSTERY
OF RELATIONSHIP

Long of limb, graceless yet,
   not quite eye to eye we meet.
Male child, first born
   not so long before.

My protector he
   though fledgling still,
The pattern clear through shadow
   of the child he used to be.

My powers wane,
   and not for long
I stem the tide of all that he will have to know;
Sad knowledge, joy and pain
   where I can never intervene.
But bond there is
   and always will be.
My son! My son!

"And he will turn the hearts of fathers to their children and the hearts of children to their fathers . . . ."

MALACHI 4:6

RELATIONSHIPS ARE WHAT LIFE IS ABOUT.

Long ago I discovered this fact in chemistry class, of all places. I cannot remember many specifics, but I can still see in my mind's eye the intricate structure of molecules diagramed to explain the formula for aspirin. Sodium acetyl salicylate, it was called, the scientific name given to the precise relationship of molecules which produces the common remedy for headaches.

This chemistry class gave me my first real glimpse of the physical structure of matter and my initial grasp of the beautiful order of the universe. As I have read about the exploration of our world—in the field of astronomy, for instance—I have been staggered by the complexity of interdependence of all matter. Molecular structure testifies to the extent to which one physical property is related to another, and indeed to all others, in the structure.

In the area of human relationships, serious study of the impact of those relationships on the individual is just beginning. There is much that we need to learn, and it is hard to acquire much really scientific knowledge, because people don't stay in one place, like molecules. People have a way of confounding scientific study, but I think a basic understanding of the effect of relationships has been part of man's knowledge about himself for a long time. The English poet John Donne (1573–1631) said it well— no man is an island. The complicated web of relationships has repeated itself in each generation since the first woman and first man decided to live together. In doing so they found themselves committed to mutual interdependence, for better or for worse. So it continues today: each of us has his own set of relationships; life consists of interaction with those people we find ourselves involved with.

Some relationships can be defined by a single word. "Daughter," "mother," "brother," "son"—these words spell out hereditary involvement. And there is only one man in the world at this given moment with whom I can be a woman in the fullest sense of the word. He is my husband. I know many other men, and I can count them as my friends, but there are things about me that are reserved for this one man alone. Certainly the sexual relationship is a clear example of this. In the eyes of society and in the sight of heaven I am joined to this man, and my expression of myself as a sexual being is worked out in relationship to him.

I have three children; and of all the children in the world, it is with these three alone that I can claim the relationship of mother. If I am to experience the joy and the pain of being a mother, I must experience it with these three. I suspect many women harbor images of dream children who are lovable, clean, tidy, well-mannered little creatures, but these images are not real children who have their growing pains, their problems, and their challenges. My responsibility in this relationship of mother is to nurture the development of these youngsters into mature adults. Anyone who thinks this is an easy task has just never been a parent!

As a Christian I can say that I believe that Christ works creatively and redemptively in my life. That rather vague generalization becomes meaningful when I say that I believe Christ works creatively and redemptively in my relationships with others. Here, in the work of reconciliation, is commitment to Christ worked out in practical terms.

Do you have a problem getting along with anyone you know? I know I do, particularly with those people who know me best. It is not hard for me to look "right" in the context of minimal contact. I can speak to a large group of people and manage to say the correct words and even radiate a certain authority and conviction. Most of us are rather adept at "faking it" in public; that is as easy as practicing the art of saying nothing much at all. We play according to the rule of conformity, and we expect others to do so also in order that we may all manage to seem reasonably normal.

121

After *The Real and Only Life* had been published and had been read by a number of people in my home town, my mother said to me, half jokingly, "Now that you've said all those things, Nancy, you'll have to be good the rest of your life!" I was staggered by the thought, because I know myself better than that. What she was really saying, though, was that now my conduct would have to look right to the people who had read my book. Well, I'm not good and I can't even look good, because there are times when I'm cross or in a hurry or just plain out of sorts. I simply cannot be sweetness and light even just some of the time. I can smile nicely throughout a long, boring meeting and come home to my family roaring like a tiger. I can usually summon my good manners and forbearance with strangers or casual friends, but my family knows the real me. Because I am so imperfect, I very much need the consoling help of the Holy Spirit in working out the problems I create for myself with those I love most. For my understanding of the good news of Christ Jesus is that I don't have to perform perfectly; I have to trust the power of God to do what I cannot manage for myself.

I erect barriers in my relationships, hindering my freedom to enjoy and care for other people. The fortress of my self-centeredness has walls which I have built word by word, moment by moment, all my life long. At some point, out of fear of rejection, out of pride or self-pity or protectiveness, I had chosen to live apart, isolated from others. The love of God has begun to open me to the reality of concern for others, but the walls crumble slowly. Love requires a vulnerability that frightens me.

One of the greatest problems I face is the difficulty of communication. I believe that real communication must begin with sensitivity, learning to listen, to hear what another human being is trying to say. I once challenged a psychiatrist to tell me what it was about him that enabled him to offer help to troubled people, and he laughingly replied, "Oh, I have three ears. With two of them I hear what you are saying, but with the third one I understand what you mean!"

I have come to appreciate the idea of the third ear. At one of the first conferences in which my husband and I participated, I was approached at the end by a woman who told me how much she enjoyed what I had said. Truthfully, my mind had already turned toward home. When she added, "I wish we'd had a chance to talk," I replied politely, "I wish so, too." It was not until we were driving home that her quiet statement hit me. I thought, "You fool! She wanted to talk to you, right then, but you turned her away politely." I couldn't undo my mistake, but I learned. I need to listen and I need to hear.

There is something important in catching the moment, for the meaningful moments never repeat themselves in quite the same way. Particularly with children does one need to communicate when they are willing and eager; a very wise mother some years ago advised me to be home in the afternoon when my older children arrived from school. Not only do I offer cookies and milk, but I can participate in the excitement of what went on that day at school. About five minutes is the time they share with me before they go charging out of the house again, but that five minutes won't wait, any more than my children will wait to grow up.

These last few years I have tried to share my faith in Christ in a real way with my youngsters, and this has meant some Bible reading and a lot of conversation, usually at inopportune moments. One night Bob and I returned from a Bible study group, all aglow with fellowship and very pleasantly sleepy. I stuck my head in my son's room to check on him, and found that, although it was about eleven o'clock, Greg was still awake. I went to his bed to kiss him goodnight and he said, "Mother, who are the Jews?" I thought, "Oh, Greg, not now!" But then I thought again. And so I sat down beside him and began to talk about the fascinating history of God's chosen people, beginning with Abraham and continuing to the culmination of Jesus' birth. I'm not sure how much of it was clear to him, but I enjoyed telling that remarkable story again. It was a captured moment of real communication.

Dialogue, or verbal interplay, depends on acknowledgement of the value of the other person's point of view. Many conversations are simply extended monologues which shut out the words and meanings we do not wish to hear. Most political arguments are like this; sadly, many religious discussions are, too. Have you ever finished a sentence for someone? Supplied the word for which the speaker was groping? I do it almost unconsciously sometimes, because my mind is quick with words—I have a ready supply for my own needs and for the needs of others as well. It's not only rude of me, but terribly insulting to the other person. I am saying to him, "I already know what you are about to say. As a matter of fact I can say it better than you!" God help me to remember the value of each person so that what he has to say will have real meaning for me.

Above all, though, if I am to communicate with another, I must offer something of myself, with a vulnerability that is not a natural trait for human beings. Some people will upon first acquaintance tell you all their secrets but not really give of themselves. Honesty about oneself demands consideration for the sensibilities of others and a sharing of the quality of spirit that makes you different from all other souls in God's world.

I learned to be open about my own feelings in several small groups of people who gathered for that purpose. One of these was a psychotherapy group; we got pretty honest, but there was little real compassion among us for the feelings we were all expressing. We were all so busy airing our own feelings that we scarcely heard others. The group did afford me some help in overcoming my inability to express hostility; in the group I felt that it was all right to do so, because everyone else was! At first our conversation was dominated by polite nothings, but as we gradually stripped them away, our honesty became abrasive. Some time later my husband and I joined a Bible study group, the first of many to which we were to belong. In this warm group of rather new Christians (sprinkled with some very seasoned ones, wise in the faith) I found the love and genuine concern which allowed me to relax into admission of my own spiritual and emotional needs. Because these people were honest about themselves, our friendship has endured through time and separation.

Most of us at least assent to the proposition that we are unique in outlook, ability, heredity, and environment. But we habitually succumb to the temptation of trying to remake others in our own image. We feel comfortable with those who are like us, and we do not hesitate to try to pour others into our mold. Much of the revolt of adolescence centers in the hostility children feel at being pushed and shoved into the plans and dreams of their parents. Have you ever known a father who pushed his son to perform in sports, not as the father had done, but even better? Or a mother whose social climbing involved having a perfect little lady for a daughter?

But neither are children free of the desire to rearrange their parents. I have found myself guilty of trying to organize my mother's life, now that she is a widow. With some very fine intentions, I set out to encourage her to "do things." She didn't want to "do things"; she wanted to live her life the way she had for some time. I began to understand that I should try to be sensitive to her real needs. I found that she didn't want me to take her to concerts—she never had cared much about music. She wanted me to have lunch with her and her friends, who were feeling a bit by-passed in the swish of suburban child-centered society.

And as I have begun to recognize my tendency to want people the way I think they should be, I have become aware of the power struggle that can go on in a marriage between a man and a woman—two very different creatures, to be sure. I was about twelve years old when it first dawned on me that little boys did not think quite like little girls, and I've been amazed ever since, although I hope I have grown in understanding. Male and female do not think alike and they do not react emotionally in the same way. And furthermore, it does seem that opposites attract, so a marriage usually involves great temperamental variations as well. In this close relationship the differences are accentuated, and the struggle for supremacy of type is on. For example, I come from a reading family; nice people always read, not just magazines, but *books*. I was appalled to discover after our marriage that my husband was not a reader. He did things, he created, he talked to people, he learned things; but he didn't read anything much that I could see. I have nagged and pleaded and coaxed and cried, but fifteen years later he still doesn't read much. Why should he, really? Because he ought to be like me and like my father and like my grandmother and all those other readers in my heritage? Thank goodness he isn't like me, for I have learned much from him that isn't in books, and he has kept me actively in the mainstream of life where it's happening.

What often happens, then, in relationships is that we not only wish to change others, or to impose our will upon theirs, but we do not hesitate to use many forms of emotional blackmail in order to do so. A woman endures an unhappy marriage for the sake of the children; only she expects her children to recognize her sacrifice and reward her with perpetual devotion. A man defies his church and family to marry a woman not of his faith; he may then come to feel that she must make it up to him—that now she must compensate him for his loss of family, of God,

127

of his way of life. This is conditional love—"I have sacrificed for you; now you *must* love me forever!" And lest we be scornful of such a love, I must add that, in my opinion all human love is conditional; it must be so. Push my love far enough, do the unforgivable, and you will find what conditions are attached. I love my son, but it is easier for me to love him as my clean-cut son than as an outrageous looking hippie. I think I have the right to attach my own standards to the meaning of a relationship, as long as I recognize just that—that they are *my* standards and perhaps not another's. Children know the subtle conditions attached to what they need most, and most of them perform accordingly. Again I say that this is life, but even so, a child needs as often as possible to experience love without strings. I can do this in small ways and still give my children the freedom to grow, with which comes the opportunity to find out who they are, apart from me. "Be a good boy and Mommy will love you" is implied, if not stated, in most of a parent's contact with his child.

But children can turn the tables sometimes. When a child screams in rage to his parent, "I hate you!", it is a shocking time for both. The parent doesn't want his own flesh to hate him, and the child is afraid of what will happen, now that he has said the forbidden. He isn't, in most cases, expressing a real emotion. What he is really saying is, "I'm mad, because you won't let me have my way and I *want* it!" It is hard to keep from letting him have his way in the face of the terrible word "hate," but he is just practicing a little emotional blackmail. Unfortunately, this trait is found in many of us overgrown children who still want our way. We must have it, even in the face of the knowledge that it will harm us in the long run. One of life's saddest spectacles is a little girl of fifty who feels that the world is denying her her rightful share of the lollipops.

Ah, but each of us is a complex package, a contradictory blend of good and bad, fragmented and whole. And who can truly know another human being? And beyond knowing, understand the kaleidoscopic images projected by him? Where do we find the psychological truth about the other half of a relationship, when we barely glimpse the truth about the one we know best, our secret self? But we have to try, for misunderstood and difficult relationships are better than being alone—a kind of premature death. God help us all—we do need each other.

THE LIMITS
OF LOVE

"... He who does not love remains in death."

I JOHN 3:14

THE PATTERN OF RELATIONSHIP INVOLVES the working out of shifting emotions and re-aligned needs. It is nice to be loved; it makes the world a bright place, and problems seem to recede as we feel ourselves accepted. One of the basic human needs is to experience this acceptance often enough to know one's own worth. Each of us must cry out, if only inside, "Love me, love me for myself alone! But don't see me as I really am, for I know that then you cannot love me." Here is the motivation for the deceptions we practice in order to be loved. We assume the burden of masks and we expend tremendous amounts of energy to fool each other.

But there is another aspect of love that involves the need to be needed. To be denied a feeling of being important to another person is to be denied a sense of value. Many of us in our middle years, our lives filled by responsibilities of homes and children and businesses, have not stopped long enough to consider the emptiness which may come when there ceases to be a bustle about life. Older people often feel that they no longer really count in the scheme of things. Each of us wants to feel that someone else depends on our strength, our wisdom, our concern. So we get to the heart of what a real relationship is all about—mutual need and mutual concern.

Does God really care that we love each other? Isn't it enough to just love God with all our hearts? I caught a glimpse of the meaning of love one night several years ago. Our little girl was about three at the time, and her older brother was eleven. Bob and I were going out for the evening; we had a new babysitter about whom Jennifer was very dubious, and she decided she was going to protest. After Bob had quieted her tears, we prepared to leave. He took our son aside and asked him to play with his sister, explaining the situation. We left, a little reluctantly, I suppose.

When we returned the sitter said that everything was fine, that the children were asleep. We looked in Jennifer's room, but she wasn't in her bed. We rushed into the boys' bedroom and sure enough, there she was, tucked into Robin's bed, sound asleep; her big brother was curled up at the foot of the bed, guarding her. Bob and I smiled at each other. At that moment we felt a surge of love for this child of ours who had done something very special for his sister.

As we talked about it that night (as fond parents do), we realized that perhaps this is something of the same kind of feeling that God must have when we love each other here on earth and try to do our best to show our concern in a real way. Again and again in the New Testament we are reminded that to love God is to love one's neighbor. Well, for me, it's easier to love God than to love all these "imperfect" people that surround me. So I must have the help of God's Holy Spirit if I am to live in the relationship of concern and service that He asks of me.

I have thought a lot about what emotions Christ must have felt on the Cross. He must have felt terrible physical pain; but I wonder if perhaps the emotional agony was not the worst part of His sacrifice. I know the extent of my own "lostness," and I have glimpsed in other people's lives the torment that separation from God brings to them. But at that point in time, Christ assumed the burden of wrongness for all the people of the world, past, present, future. Does that atonement make provision for the sins of Hitler? Of Lee Harvey Oswald? Of Paul? Of Nancy Peerman?

The Christian faith says yes! And that affirmation is great good news, because anyone who searches his heart at all must realize that he cannot by himself straighten out the twisted strands of his own behavior. What the world needs today, as always, is a Saviour; for now, as always, there is too much hate and not enough love. Because this is so, the world needs, too, those who, by their knowledge of the saving grace of God, can love others in a new and different way.

Christians are given a number of guidelines in the art

of being aware of others and their needs. The example of Christ as One who cared to the ultimate limit of life itself cannot be surpassed. Even people who do not believe in His divinity point to Him as the perfect servant of His fellowmen, although they would rob His cross of its final significance.

As a Christian, I can become very discouraged if I try to approximate the behavior of Jesus as my goal; His life had a quality about it which I can only hope will be echoed faintly in my own life. I think the example which God showed to the world in His Son was meant to tell us that this is what we are to become at some point beyond our experience here and now. Paul expressed this in the third chapter of Philippians when he spoke of not being already perfect, but of pressing on toward the goal.

The Scriptures record God's revelation of love, and they deal with the whole question of concern for the fate of others. Who can read the Sermon on the Mount without having a sinking feeling that whatever we have managed to do about loving others has been a mere token? I have forgiven someone perhaps seven times, but seventy times seven is another matter entirely. I haven't walked very many extra miles either. So I am brought back to my dependence on the spirit of God in me to enable me to love those people who annoy me, fail me, dislike me, or are otherwise not natural candidates for my affection. For instance, it is easier for me to love the afflicted than those who afflict themselves and the people around them. But God will not let me ignore those persons I would like to cross off my list, so I must struggle on with my lack of love, trusting God to provide me with what I do not now possess.

Oddly enough, my own experience has been that God uses my personal relationship with Him, my communication in prayer, as a potent means of changing my heart about another person. Prayer has a very private place in my life, but through intercession I can bring into my time with God the real concerns of others. It is hard to hold a grudge against someone when you have asked God to help this person know His love. It seems to be blasphemy to withhold what you are asking of God. If I can manage enough concern for someone to pray for him, then I believe I am on my way toward a more creative relationship with him. If I can honestly confess my real, natural feelings, God can begin to purge me of them, at least to some extent.

Perhaps the great strength in the ongoing life of a Christian is the knowledge that God has a creative purpose which continues forever. In all the circumstances of life, through pain, joy, uneasiness, loss, or happiness, the hand of God holds us to that purpose, so that for those who love God, all things do work together for good. If I believe this, then I must first trust God to be able to change a relationship. Next, though, I must be willing to act on what God shows me that I must do. There's the problem—I often don't want to exert myself that much. It's easier to turn away from someone I don't like or to keep myself at such a distance that the question of concern is never put to the test. Love without involvement is an empty promise of concern. I can talk a long, long time about love without demonstrating it in the slightest way.

137

I have known what it means to love on God's terms. I have been loved that way by others. In any relationship which God has touched there are qualities which mark the presence of the Holy Spirit. For me, acceptance, a positive step beyond tolerance, is born of the knowledge that I am God's child and the other person is His child also. Beyond acceptance is a willingness to offer love without being certain that I'll get back as much as I give. I find it hard to go out on a limb, emotionally; I might be rejected. But love without strings is a rare gift, and I want to try to give it sometimes. Knowing that God has pardoned me makes it easier for me to forgive others for real offenses, or for slights and hurts. And I do need to learn patience, both with my own shortcomings and with those of others. Some relationships improve slowly because the misunderstandings are many. I can be honest, though, in appraising what the relationship is now, as well as hoping for much more.

After all, aren't these the qualities of God's love for me? But even in this ultimate relationship of God and man, there are the same difficulties that we find in human ties. We fail to communicate with God; we remake Him in our own image; we try emotional blackmail by insisting that we know better than He does about the pattern our lives should assume. God meets our every difficulty with His free gift of love, with acceptance of each one of us, no matter where we are. He offers forgiveness of our transgressions and the healing which comes from the lifting of guilt. God knows about us and He cares.

If I give Him permission, He will show me how to live a kind of life of love and concern that I can never know by myself. There are no outer limits to God's love. In Christ He offers everything. Nor do I think that there are boundaries beyond which He does not wish His children to care. I cannot imagine that He would ever say to me, "That's enough. You have loved enough." Instead I think that His own concern for all His children pushes us to care for them more than we ever dreamed possible.

THE VISIBLE
SIGN

The time has come
And must come again
To pause,
If but for the instant;
To offer up the dirty hands,
The poorest gift.

These imperfect lips
That touch the cup
To drink of vine and summer sun,
The fullness of the seasons,
The cup of life.

For He it is
To Whom I come
Again, again,
And yet again,
To find what is lost,
If but for the instant.

"For the gifts and the call of God are irrevocable."

ROMANS 11:29

FOR ME THERE IS A KIND OF INEVITABILITY about walking up the center aisle of my church to the altar in response to the invitation to receive the Lord's Supper. It is a gathering up at a point in time of all events in life, an end and a beginning.

It is consciousness of sin and belief in forgiveness, mingled with the knowledge of just what it is that I am about to receive. No ordinary gift, this bread and wine, but the symbol of the relationship between God and man, freely offered, gladly received. Who could buy such a gift? And where? There seems to be a foretaste of heaven in such a simple meal. So it is with the life of a Christian, bound up in the here and the hereafter. He is a person set apart, living the sacramental life, richly embroidered with the things of God—people, love, prayer, the Holy Supper, food for eternity.

Growing up in the Episcopal Church I memorized the traditional definition for the word "sacrament"—an outward and visible sign of an inward and spiritual grace. But I never really thought to apply the definition to anything besides the communion service or baptism or one of the ceremonies of my church. To be truthful, it did not seem to be a very practical word; it was a word reserved for the religious segment of my life. It never occurred to me that it could have anything to do with the rest of living.

Many of us have an idea about what a "religious" life would be like, if only we had the will to live it. According to common presuppositions, it would reflect aspects such as humble living, denial of pleasure, meekness of spirit, passivity, and a certain heroic determination to eliminate human weakness. This narrow way sounds a bit boring, certainly not very contemporary, and above all a quaint side-stepping of what is happening in the world today. Because few of us seem to fit the criteria, we conclude that we cannot live the religious life, and so relegate things religious to a corner of our experience called Sunday morning.

This hardly seems to be enough, though, for some of us who have been touched by the experience of conversion or deepened by a glimpse of the kind of life that God gives in relationship to Christ. We want more of religion than a few hours a week, and so we begin the long journey of faith, seeking a life with God. But conversion or a new understanding of commitment to Christ does not bring im-

144

mediate "right" behavior, or thought, or feeling. I cannot actually see myself changing, but by the daily discipline of surrender of my will I prepare myself for change. And the steady commitment day by day produces a different quality of character, for God is building within me someone I may scarcely recognize in the end. That person will be the one which God Himself creates; not the someone I have created out of my own imaginings and wishes.

When a Christian remains doggedly devoted to his Lord, in spite of temptation, in spite of sin, in spite of the continuing resurrection of selfish desire, then that Christian has the promises of God that He will complete what He has begun. I look at myself and I get discouraged. I know my secret transgressions, and yet, looking a second time, I can acknowledge that I am now a different person than I was before I knew Christ Jesus.

A disciple, after all, is simply one who accepts and follows a teacher or a doctrine. I can be a disciple of Freud or of Marshall McLuhan or of yoga or of any one of a thousand other people or ideas. But if I choose to become a disciple at all, then I must reckon the cost in terms of what will be required of me. A disciple is produced by discipline, for though the word sometimes has the connotation of punishment, it actually means systematic training or subjection to authority, the habit of obedience. To be a disciple of the Lord Jesus means that I surrender myself in obedience to the will of God. I couple the words "surrender" and "obedience," for they are the two sides of the same coin—my will.

I might just as well confess, right here, that systematic

145

anything goes against my natural grain. Perhaps as a child I had sufficient freedom to try a great many things without submitting my total time and effort to any one of them. My enthusiasms have been great (and often brief) so the word "discipline" is a frightening one for me. I suppose this is one of the reasons that I am so grateful that God has made provision in His kingdom for such undisciplined souls as me. I need the gift of the Spirit of God, imparted to me by my relationship with Christ. Now I have no final excuse for my lack of obedience, for the Spirit Himself works within me to produce what God asks of me.

I know that at a certain moment of my life I offered to God the right to my soul. I did so, partly because He seemed to be my only hope for a life of sanity and wholeness in the midst of a world I did not understand. In return, I had the assurance of the Word of God that He would honor my commitment by His faithfulness "for he has said, 'I will never fail you nor forsake you' " (Hebrews 13:5). Often I choose to behave in a self-centered way, but I know that in the long run my selfishness will yield to God. Once and for all Christ settles the problem of being human; there is no possibility of ultimate defeat for me.

It is not so much that the specific circumstances of my life have changed as a result of my commitment of my life to Christ but the order of importance has changed, and my value system, too. Time, money, talent, friends, family—I don't have a new set of them. Rather, these things and people that give shape to my life are beginning to look different to me.

146

My husband and I, from the earliest days of our marriage have led a busy social life. Now that our lives have been reoriented to Christ, we have not eliminated parties and the people who go to them, but social occasions have a different emphasis in the total view of our lives together. Someone once asked me at what point in my Christian life I had given up my old friends. I'm sure she didn't quite mean it to sound as harsh as it did, but the implication of her question shocked me nevertheless. I answered quite honestly that we had never consciously cut the cord of friendship with any of the people who had been "pre-Christian" friends. Some of them are now "Christian" friends, for they, too, have found reality in knowing Christ. Some others think we are a bit soft in the head on religion, but they don't really mind and we love them still.

Certainly we have new friendships which are bonds in Christ. And while there is no question that we spend our time differently now, I hope we never come to a time when it's "us guys" and "those others." In fact, I love to give dinner parties, because I feel that the use of my home and my talents as a hostess can be an offering to God and a pleasant introduction to Christ for some people who wouldn't be caught dead in church.

There are practical ways in which the Holy Spirit changes things, for instance, in the use of time. Time is a precious commodity, limited, a gift the value of which is sometimes overlooked. Almost everyone seems to have either too much of it or too little. For some, time hangs heavy on hands that have ceased to be productive or useful.

I have seen the terrible toll taken by the loss of a sense of worth in older people who no longer feel needed.

For many of us, though, who are not yet at that stage of life, there seems to be an ever-decreasing amount of time in which to do an ever-increasing amount of work—the old trap of the treadmill. I have often marveled at the almost ceaseless activity of my three children, who seem determined to make every moment count with Scouts and school-work and tennis and games—and arguments, when there is nothing better to do. Their energy overwhelms me. But then I think about their father—an architectural designer, builder, weekend painter, and tennis player, who is also interested in listening to music and watching football games. I must further reflect with a laugh that their mother belongs to clubs, teaches art as a volunteer, plays compulsive tennis, loves to read, enjoys doing creative stitchery, and is in the midst of writing a second book, in between car pools. In our family, as in most, the wonder is that we all get along so well, in view of the fact that we are spreading ourselves too thin in all directions for a twenty-four-hour day.

There are many of us who share a sense of frustration about all the things we would like to do, ought to do, and never manage to do. I have had to learn that there is a negative aspect to the creative expenditure of time. What is to be my answer to the demands (most of them worthwhile) that people, causes, and organizations make on my limited supply of minutes and hours? It is a problem without a ready solution.

Ministers face this time dilemma to a heart-breaking

degree; we all expect so much of them. At a church meeting one night after Bob and I had finished speaking, we asked for questions. The young minister shot up his hand. He said, "Listen, how can I do all that I should for my people, and not be a stranger to my own wife and son? How do you say no to people who really are in need?" I thought a moment, and I realized that *I* didn't have the answer. I could say, though, that in seeking to work out God's plan for my own life, I had found the courage to say no firmly, even at the risk of sometimes offending someone. Personally, I have come to feel that the best, if not always the most, of my time belongs to those persons God has given me in close relationship. One of the real dangers in Christian work for the layman (and the professional) is that he may seek to win the world for Christ and lose his own children.

As a woman, a wife, and a mother, I try to apportion my time in concentric circles, with the inmost circle belonging to my family. The outer circles are arranged in light of the particular circumstances God has allowed to come into my life at the time. At one point it may seem that work in my church is most important; or that leading a prayer group may be what I need to do; or that working for the United Fund should take precedence. As I have watched others in their civic, social and religious activities, the most effective people seem to be those who fit their own talents to certain jobs and then give their best to those few jobs.

Even if I am careful, my schedule can get over-extended. I am sure my bank would take a dim view of me if I were as careless with my money as I sometimes am with my time! I have wasted many frustrating days wondering how I could possibly get to all the meetings to which I was committed. I worried about all that I had to do, past, present and future. My husband faces the same situation in his business—concurrent appointments, overlapping meetings, too many phone calls—but he has found real help from God.

At dinner one evening he mentioned all the problems and catastrophes that had confronted him that day, and I wondered aloud how he managed to seem so fresh and relaxed. He said, "You know, I committed everything as it came along and God gave me the insight to see that what I needed to do was to concentrate completely on each thing as it arose. I didn't look back and I didn't try to run ahead of the present moment. I got everything done and I'm not even tired." Surely this is creative use of time as God would have it, but often I refuse to pause long enough to consider the eternity of the moment. Sometimes I think I really love my own confusion, because at least it proves I'm *doing* something!

Beyond the misuse of time, one of the great wastes in life is that of potential never realized. Admittedly, talents are not distributed equally to everyone, but each of us has potential which must be forced into bloom. My husband and I were talking one evening with a young man who had just returned from army service and was going back to college. He was suffering from vocational frustration; he wasn't sure what he ought to be preparing to do in life, but he felt strongly his need to contribute to society.

This seemed to be a rather abstract desire, so we talked awhile about social needs, future development of technology, and so on. While we were discussing all this, suddenly I thought, "Perhaps making a contribution to society is as simple as being yourself to the fullest extent possible." I tried to explain to Charlie my flash of insight. I found that because he didn't have a very favorable image of himself he couldn't believe that this could be so for him. I guess he felt that there was not much potential to fulfill. For the Christian who wants to do God's will, a sacramental life may not mean giving up things, but accepting possibilities.

Several years ago my husband and I were invited to participate in a weekend conference at Laity Lodge, a retreat center near Leakey, Texas. It was a time of real pleasure for us both because a year earlier we had found a vital relationship with Christ at a similar conference there. Now we both were to give a witness to what had happened to us in the time since. Before the actual speaking time arrived, I had been very nervous, but now I was through with my part of the program and was sitting on a porch in the warm sunshine, listening to a small group of people discuss the book of Romans. To be truthful, I felt a little smug, for things were going well in my life now after much previous emotional turmoil. Besides, I had been studying the Bible and I already understood the difficult bit of theology with which one woman was struggling.

In the midst of my complacency it was as though someone suddenly tapped me on the shoulder and said, "Nancy, you're tiptoing around about all this!" I was startled because it was so unexpected, but I thought, "That's right. What would happen if you put no limits on what God could do with your time and talents?" I felt very uneasy, for I knew that I was being urged on to a situation where perhaps I would not feel so comfortable. I was afraid, because I suspected something more difficult was going to be required of me.

During the conference, I talked with a friend of some spiritual maturity about my feeling, and he wisely advised me to accept my insight without stretching it too much. He suggested that God was perhaps preparing me for something, and that my part was to accept, at this present moment, the possibility that God wanted to use me in a new way. I was willing to do that, for I wanted to be part of God's work in the world. About two months later Bob and I received our first invitation to witness at a large church meeting. My fear of having to speak in front of two thousand people was overcome by the knowledge that God was asking me to trust Him, not to hold back. The possibility became reality; God had prepared me to acknowledge Him publicly, in spite of my reluctance to be open about myself with more than a few people at a time.

As Christians we share a heavy responsibility, urged upon us by Christ when He told His disciples to go out into the world, teaching and baptizing. He said, in effect, that Christians must share their faith; it is not enough to believe and understand and then keep it to oneself. But it is hard to tell the world about Christ, at least it always seems hard for me to do so. The world is full of skeptical and weary people who have experienced too much of the failure of idealism to believe readily in salvation of any kind. But because Christ has made a real difference in my life, I have to try; I see so many people around me who have the same needs that I have.

Witness in its most effective sense is sharing your life with others so that they can identify with you. People may admire saints but they don't reveal their weaknesses to them—they can't believe that those saints *ever* experienced the difficulties in which they find themselves. The purpose of the Christian witness is to point the way to Christ, so that those who wish to find Him may do so. One of the hardest lessons I have to learn is that my witness never convérted anyone; God's Holy Spirit does the converting! So the results—the "success" or "failure" of a witness— are not in my hands. My responsibility is to pray, pray, pray; to be obedient to the opportunities that come; to tell the truth about Christ; and to leave the rest to God.

The only way to keep the gift which God has given to you is to spend and be spent. Lavish love and never stop to count the cost. I had a dream one night, in which I clearly saw a man whom I knew, Joe Blinco. Joe was a member of the Billy Graham team and he had meant much to me as a teacher and guide. Joe was a glorious preacher, and in my dream I heard him say quite clearly, in his wonderful voice, "God's grace becomes God's judgment!" I woke suddenly, and ever since I have pondered the meaning of those words. I think it is a way of saying that the measure which you have been given is the measure which you must offer to others.

I truly know the healing which God has freely offered

me. I have experienced the joy of knowing Him, even if I perceive Him only dimly. I have trusted Him with the outcome of my life, here and forever. What should be my response to all that He has given me? Not fear, certainly; perhaps gratitude and a sense of thanksgiving. But more than that, perhaps the willingness to go on with Him. I have to say to myself, "All right, my girl; I know there are times when you think you'll never make it! Perhaps the glow of conversion was an illusion after all. It's life as usual now, the long haul, and the glamour has worn off. Well, the relationship between you and God is not that fragile; once created, it cannot be severed. You may turn your back, or try to, but you will be haunted by God forever."

I guess you get what you really want. The discipline of desire is to get what you want to have through acceptance of what is possible. To know who you are, really—this gives great strength to whatever you set out to do. To know God gives you great confidence, for your life bears the seal of the Holy Spirit for all eternity. To live your life as an offering to God is to succeed, whatever happens.

Lord, at this moment, it is my intent to do Thy will, until the very end.

Amen—so let it be.

CLASS		ACC

Peerman, Nancy

(LAST NAME OF AUTHOR)

Seasons of the Soul

(BOOK TITLE)

DATE DUE	ISSUED TO